£5.95p

THE
PERSONAL
GROWTH
HANDBOOK

GW00725843

*Other books by Liz Hodgkinson
published by Piatkus*

The Alexander Technique
Codependency (with David Stafford)
Obsessive Love
Reincarnation: The Evidence
Spiritual Healing

THE
PERSONAL
GROWTH
HANDBOOK

*Dozens of ways
to develop your inner self*

LIZ HODGKINSON

PIATKUS

© 1993 Liz Hodgkinson

First published in 1993 by
Judy Piatkus (Publishers) Ltd of
5 Windmill Street, London W1P 1HF

**The moral right of the author
has been asserted**

*A catalogue record for this book is
available from the British Library*

ISBN 0–7499–1215–4

Edited by Carol Franklin
Designed by Sue Ryall
Cover by Jennie Smith

Set in 11/13 Linotron Ehrhardt by
Phoenix Photosetting, Chatham
Printed and bound in Great Britain by
Bookcraft Ltd, Midsomer Norton

Contents

PART 1

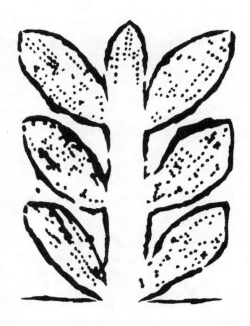

PART 1

Chapter 1

What is Personal Growth?

My Own Story

As with many people, my own journey towards personal growth – which I don't see as being anywhere near finished yet – started apparently by accident.

It was 1977, and I was working as a journalist on the *People* newspaper. At the time, my life was hectic, fun and highly paid. I loved the whole life – the three-hour lunch breaks, the exciting stories, the hours spent sitting in pubs, the camaraderie, the gossip, the bouts of intensely hard work, the pleasure I felt when my story made the front page. I'd always wanted to work on a national newspaper, and here I was actually working on one. As one of the few young women in the editorial department at the time – long before the days when one could even imagine a tabloid editor being female – I was used to being asked out to lunch, fêted and chatted up.

At the same time as having a glamorous and sometimes nerve-wracking job – such as when people who don't want their stories too closely investigated chased us off their premises, or threatened to smash cameras – I had a happy home life as well. I was married to a journalist on *The Times*, and we had two beautiful young sons and a roomy, five-bedroomed house in Richmond. We drove a Morgan sports car, had foreign holidays, lots of good friends and truly seemed to have it all.

The fact that this lifestyle didn't lead to any kind of personal growth –

1

except around the waistline if you weren't very, very careful (but then one could always go on a free visit to a health farm) – didn't bother me at all. I was young, seemingly successful, and with both of us earning high salaries, we had money to spend and to spare.

I certainly wasn't looking for any change or insights about myself. So far as I was concerned I was perfect, living the ideal, high-achieving life. Then, things began to happen which, without my perhaps being fully aware of it, were to affect my life and ideas dramatically.

Every now and again, the newspaper would hold a sale of books which had been sent in during the year, for charity. Mostly, these sales consisted of titles nobody wanted or could sell as review copies, and so it was rare to come across one you actually felt like buying, even for a few pence. But I saw one with an intriguing title – *Your Erroneous Zones*, by American psychologist Wayne Dyer. I bought it.

That night, I started reading it in bed and, as I read on, every word seemed to be a revelation, written for me alone. Dr Dyer informed me that I didn't need to have other people's approval, that I didn't need to feel guilt or worry, that I could actually choose whether to be happy or unhappy. I did not need to be swayed by the emotional blackmail of other people. I could choose to have a positive self-image.

As I read through the book, I thought: this is true! I don't have to feel guilt and shame! I don't have to worry about anything! I don't have to feel self-pity! When I had finished the book I realised that my life and attitudes weren't perhaps as perfect as I had thought. I did often get angry and blame it on other people. I did often worry, and feel guilt. The realisation that I had no need to feel any of these negative emotions, and that I could choose not to be burdened by them was like walking from darkness into light.

But there was a long way to go. During my years at the *People* I had developed into a heavy drinker and smoker, and lover of expensive restaurants and meals out. I'd always told myself that I enjoyed smoking, and that I could give it up if I wanted to, but I didn't want to. The reality was that I was completely hooked, so much so that I lived in fear and dread of running out of cigarettes.

This happened once, in difficult circumstances. All four of us – my then husband and two sons – were staying with some friends in the country over one New Year's Eve. A party for about fifty people had been arranged, but throughout the day it snowed so heavily that, one by one, guests rang to say they couldn't make it. In the end, only one intrepid couple braved the snow and arrived at the party.

2

What is Personal Growth?

We ourselves were due to leave the next day, but could not get out because of the snow. As the day drew on, my hostess and I became increasingly nervous as we knew we did not have enough cigarettes to last us for the next twenty-four hours. We eked them out as much as we could, but by 6 p.m. we had run out completely. What to do? There was nothing for it but to take a couple of torches and try to find our way to the nearest pub – an easy journey of about a mile in ordinary conditions.

We trudged through Scott of the Antarctic conditions, terrified that we would step into a ditch, as the blanket of snow had blotted out every landmark. Eventually, after about two hours, we arrived at the pub and bought our cigarettes. We were out for four hours altogether, and came back to our smug spouses, who had given up smoking years before, and who had absolutely refused to go out for us.

When, a couple of days later, the snow had melted enough for the roads to be opened up, I thought how ridiculous it was to be so hooked on smoking that I would actually risk my life just to get cigarettes. So, I tried to give up. I would say that without doubt, it is the most difficult thing I have ever done in my entire life.

I panicked at the thought of not having one with my morning coffee, on the tube, when I sat down to work – by this time I was working at the *Daily Mail* – and really felt I needed my fags. If the mornings were difficult enough to get through, lunchtimes were a sheer nightmare. I had been in the habit of going to a nearby wine bar at lunchtime, and with my newspaper colleagues, enjoyed glasses of wine and cigarettes.

Sitting in the wine bar without a cigarette was sheer torture. I had to refuse dinner party invitations, as I did not see how I would ever sit through one without regularly lighting up. I felt as if life was simply not worth living. If I can't have my cigarettes, then I might as well just die, I thought. I looked back to the halcyon days of smoking compared to the bleak ones I lived now.

Clearly, I had to make some significant changes to my life. Going into pubs or even restaurants at lunchtime or after work was no longer a possibility, as I could not seem to enjoy either the drink or the company without a permanent cigarette in my hands. So, I joined a nearby aerobics class. This was also terrible torture, because when I put on a leotard, I realised that the years of heavy eating and drinking had left my body unattractively flabby. Suddenly, there seemed so much work to do on myself.

I had to address three areas – my emotions and attitudes, my addiction to smoking and my physical health and fitness. I had already made a start through reading Wayne Dyer's book, but I could not put this good advice into proper action until I had cleaned up my act in other areas.

Gradually, very gradually, the craving for smoking subsided until all that was left was a desire to smoke a cigarette after a really good meal. I zapped this one by smoking small cigars instead for a while, and eventually, even the wish to light up a cigar faded. Three months after making my decision, I could call myself a non-smoker. I have never smoked a cigarette since, in all those years. The sense of personal empowerment this achievement gave me meant that I was now free to look at other areas of my life, and see what could be done to improve them.

I can't say that I ever enjoyed the exercise classes I went to when trying to separate myself from smoking. I felt I looked horrible in a leotard, while all the other people there seemed to be professional dancers or models with wonderful bodies, and I've never known time tick by so slowly. We're told to love our bodies, but in my case, this was a pretty difficult job. I could only love a much nicer body than the one I had.

Exercise could only do so much: I now had to look at my diet. Over the years, I had become very greedy indeed, often eating two big restaurant meals a day. I loved Indian, Chinese, Greek, Italian, French food, and one of the greatest treats of my life was eating out. On an expense account, this is an easy enough thing to do. How do they know whether or not you've been entertaining a close contact? So, with the newspapers paying, I ate myself into an overweight, cellulite-laden slob.

At the time I had just started specialising in health writing, and messages were coming through from ever more research that a vegetarian diet could halve the risk of cancer, stabilise weight and rejuvenate body systems. My husband and myself decided to try and go vegetarian.

If smoking was the most difficult thing I've ever given up in my life, giving up meat and fish was certainly the easiest. We took it very gradually, cutting out first pork, then red meat, then chicken, then fish and, finally, eggs. I can honestly say that I have never once missed meat or fish or craved any dish that contains them. We learned to our delight that vegetarian food was actually much nicer than dishes containing animal produce. Also, as I ate healthier foods, my desire to drink so much diminished. My skin improved and I lost the excess weight.

It seemed that vegetarianism, along with the exercise and lack of smoking gave me some kind of mental clarity, so I then began investigating yoga and meditation. Going to courses and seminars helped me to gain a new perspective on life, and the messages I had received when reading Wayne Dyer's book were underlined by what the Eastern spiritual movements were saying. I felt for the first time that I was beginning to take control of my life.

And gradually, the hedonistic, high-octane life I had been leading as a daily newspaper journalist did not seem so attractive. It did not seem to nurture me. It wasn't that I wanted to give up work, or work any less hard, but perhaps a different kind of approach would now suit me better. I found the courage to go freelance – giving up that salary and those expenses was hard, but I found I actually made more money than I had been earning on my staff jobs.

Now that I no longer had to go into an office every day, I had the freedom to explore ideas which for so long had stayed on the back burner. I avidly, and somewhat belatedly, read books on feminism, and realised that all the apparent choices I had made were within patriarchal systems. I had been apparently snug and secure within my own little nuclear family, but this wasn't what I really wanted. I had got married, produced children and bought houses – all in a cloud of unknowing.

It was at this point, I think, that the struggle towards personal growth became really painful. If I was to put all my new ideas into practice, it would mean the destruction of my cosy lifestyle. Yet, it was all becoming a prison. In particular, I began to feel that compulsory marital sex was keeping me down, curtailing my freedom. It was at about this time that my then husband and myself attended a yoga course which recommended celibacy as a way of life for both single and married people. It seemed a peculiar idea to us, but as we were having such problems in our sex lives at the time, we decided to give it a try.

We moved into separate bedrooms, and gave sex a rest. The feeling of freedom and autonomy that this decision gave was so heady it was like being able to see after a lifetime of being blind. I felt that I reclaimed myself, that I was now truly liberated. Few other people seemed to be able to understand this decision, but for me it was the most empowering one I have ever made.

I never had sex again with my husband, although we were together for another eight or nine years before deciding to separate. My head was by now becoming extremely clear. I'd given up smoking, become more physically active, looked years younger, and had taken to the vegetarian diet. But there was more work to be done. I began to investigate seriously the Eastern ideas of karma, reincarnation and non-attachment, and decided they all made logical sense, even if they could not be conclusively proved.

Taking on board these ideas made me have a greater sense of responsibility towards myself, and towards other people. I became very careful of the friendships and relationships I set in motion. I also came to realise that life, instead of being random and chaotic as is often thought, is actually ordered and logical, like a jewelled movement. Whatever we put out, we get back.

But there was no room for complacency. I still did not love my body, even though it had improved somewhat since going vegetarian. But I now decided to try and get rid of the accumulated cellulite on my thighs, something I had always hated and which made me feel sick and ill every time I looked at it. Eventually I managed it, and this also increased confidence in myself. Other physical improvements I made were to have 'Hollywood nails' and breast augmentation. All these gave me a sense of taking charge of my body, not just leaving it to Mother Nature who, as we all know, is monstrously unfair in her distribution of physical attributes.

The body therapies I tried made me realise that you do not have to 'let yourself go' at a certain age, but that with hard work and dedication, you can keep slim and supple and healthy much longer than most people ever imagine.

For me, the journey eventually meant I had to live on my own, reclaim myself, fulfil my personal destiny. So I got divorced, established myself in my own flat and realised, to my satisfaction, that I could do everything for myself – redecorate my flat, see to my garden, look after my car, earn my own living (which I had always done anyway) and, also, bring the male and female sides of my character together. I realised with joy that I did not need somebody else to 'complete' me, since I was already complete in myself.

Another powerful anaesthetic – that of having a permanent partner in my life – was off. Life is not always comfortable without anybody else automatically there, but how wonderful it is to know that I can be self-reliant in everything, that I never need to depend on anybody else to be 'there' for me. My new life means that I can come and go exactly as I please, without having anybody else to consider.

So much do I value my freedom that I would never have even a pet animal to look after, or anything which would curtail my ability to make instant decisions regarding my life and whereabouts.

I also, along the way, had to face the pain of my past. This, I would say, has been the most agonising aspect of my own journey towards personal growth. It included unearthing and coming to terms with a highly traumatic and unrequited early love affair – something for which I needed professional therapy – and trying to come to terms with some nightmare aspects of my childhood; the realisation that I had come from an alcoholic, non-supportive and non-nurturing background, where I felt responsible for my parents, rather than the other way round.

For most of my adult life I had shoved this into the background and refused to think about it. But it, too, had to be faced if I was to be freed from the prison of the past.

I can't say that it's all over, that all is now guaranteed peace and contentment. All the time, new lessons have to be learned. For instance, when I moved into my present flat, I was earning a lot of money and had just sold my previous house for a huge profit. I was feeling very confident, and I employed a professional interior designer and chose the most expensive and lavish equipment and furnishings for my flat, believing that I deserved the best.

I had the garden landscaped. I had a cleaning lady. I sent all my sheets to the laundry. I travelled. I bought vintage champagne – no, I haven't become a teetotaller, although some people do on the personal growth path. I lived the life of a rich person. The only problem was that I wasn't rich, and I got poorer and poorer and more panic-stricken as my income plummeted at the same time as house prices fell and mortgage rates rocketed. It was all extremely uncomfortable and a reminder that we all have to be prepared for whatever might happen.

If I'd stuck to my job at the *People*, had continued to live the life of an expense-account hedonist, I would probably never have had these last few years of comparative poverty and high stress over money. But at the same time, I would never have gained the insights that have enabled me to research and to write this book, the insights which have given me a new serenity and peace in myself, and made the outside world seem a far more friendly and loving place than I had previously imagined.

My own journey has enabled me to meet some wonderful people, take part in exciting travel and explore frontiers of knowledge and ideas which would otherwise have been sealed off. It has enabled me to let go of many negative emotions, of hostility, resentment, anger and guilt, and take on board more loving and positive ones.

I now have no enemies at all – at least, I don't think I have. I don't hate anybody, and feel that nobody hates me. The fact that I have not embarked on intimate, exclusive relationships means that I have more time and freedom to cultivate friendships. So now I can go out alone, with a friend or with a group – I'm not eternally glued to the same person wherever I go.

To some people, it may seem that I have lost more than I've gained. I'm living alone, I have lost my husband and my marriage, and have no expectations of ever putting that lifestyle back together again.

So how does what has happened to me constitute personal growth? Does it always have to be painful, and involve giving things up? Some people might not even be able to imagine that they could be happy not eating rich meals, and drinking and smoking, or having regular sex.

I see personal growth in rather the same way as learning a new language, or a musical instrument. The path might seem easy at first, but at some stage you are going to come up against difficulties. It is how you tackle those difficulties that determines the measure of growth. And with every obstacle and stepping-stone that is overcome, the reward will be greater inner peace, greater contentment, greater creativity – and the chance to fulfil your own personal potential to the utmost.

You've read a brief resumé of my story. I will now try to explain a little further what I understand by the term 'personal growth', and why I believe it is the most important, most exciting and most rewarding journey we can ever make.

Basically, personal growth is all about self-discovery. It is about finding out exactly what kind of person you are, and what you really want out of life, rather than what others might want for you, or what society might expect from you.

When we 'grow', we become more self-aware. We are able to take responsibility for ourselves and our actions, and can start to see the rest of humanity as our brothers, sisters and friends, rather than as enemies or strangers.

We also become happier in ourselves, at peace, and are able to move forward in a purposeful way of our own choosing, rather than being buffeted this way and that by other people's desires and emotions. When we grow, we become strong in ourselves, masters and mistresses of our own fate, and also more flexible. We become aware that nothing in this world is permanent, that everything is subject to change, and we understand that any material possession we have, any close relationship, can be snatched away from us at any minute. We learn not to overvalue material goods, but to become strong in ourselves so that we can manage without them, if necessary.

When we grow, we are able to become the very best of ourselves. Our true character can shine out, unclouded by negative emotions, doubts, fears, worries. We become strong, self-reliant, independent, autonomous, able to take charge of our lives.

Perhaps this all sounds very nice, and universally desirable. Yet, believe it or not, the whole concept of personal growth has had – and is having – a very hard time becoming accepted as a goal worth aiming at. Since the term 'personal growth' first appeared, along with the human potential movement in the 1960s, it has been sneered at, ridiculed as navel-gazing, selfish, narcissistic and irrelevant to the problems of society at large. Instead of looking inwards, detractors point out, we should be seeking to correct the ills of society, to make sure nobody is poverty-stricken or homeless.

This book is written from the point of view that, before we start to look at society's problems, we have to look at ourselves and get our own house in order. Then we will be in a position to affect the society we live in, to its betterment. As I see it, personal growth is something none of us can afford to ignore, if we truly want to make the best of ourselves, our surroundings, our society and our relationships.

The question is: exactly how do we go about maximising our potential, and becoming wise and self-aware?

There is no easy or foolproof route, no instant enlightenment, and some of the paths may lead nowhere, or just peter out. But that is all part of the journey, all part of the learning process. And nowadays there are many organisations and movements which can help us to hack a path through the jungle of thoughts, emotions, ideas, aspirations and hopes which go to make each one of us individual and human, and can provide at least some sort of guide along the route.

But as there are so many paths, so many movements, organisations and offshoots, how does the eager aspirant ever start such a journey? How are any of us to know what might be right for us, what sort of commitment we ought to give and, also, when we have 'grown'?

And that is where this book comes in. It has been written for all those who may have become curious about the personal growth movement, for everybody who has ever asked themselves: could it be for me?

It is for people who vaguely feel there may be something missing in their lives, without perhaps knowing exactly what this is; for those who feel that their lives are purposeless and without meaning, for everybody who may want to change aspects of their lives or their personalities but has no idea of how to go about it. It is, above all, for those people who are willing and ready to take charge of their lives, and not to be victims any more.

Very many people, it must be said, feel highly suspicious of the whole personal growth movement, and imagine that it is full of cranks and charlatans on the one hand and ineffectual hippy types on the other, with nothing in between. In fact, although suspicious characters and spurious movements do exist, they are in the minority. Most of the organisations and movements, in order to have lasted, are genuine, although not all may resonate with you, of course.

I hope this guide will serve to allay your doubts and suspicions, and also to shed light on what the personal growth movement is all about, that is, gaining valuable insights into ourselves, insights which help us to live our lives more fully and purposefully than before.

A Brief History of the Personal Growth Movement

In order to be able to put it into perspective, it is important to understand just how the whole personal growth movement started – and why.

In the first place, there is nothing new about wanting to understand and know oneself. Since the beginning of time, people have sought to maximise their potential, to understand the meaning of life, and to try and discover where they came from, where they are going and why they are here. But in the past, this search has been confined mainly to those who have had the leisure and education for it – a small minority of people for most of history.

Until the middle of the twentieth century, almost the only people who asked themselves serious, searching questions about the meaning of life were poets, philosophers and those engaged on a spiritual quest, people whose lives were devoted to trying to wrest some meaning from their existence. They were the geniuses, the seers, the few, the privileged. For the majority, life was a matter of sheer survival, and most people did not have much say in their own destiny.

The great majority of us did not have the opportunity to ask deep and difficult questions. For one thing, it was unlikely that we could have come up with any proper answers and, for another, it was so hard simply to scrape together even the bare necessities for living that we would hardly have known how to ask the questions anyway.

When life is a constant struggle to earn enough money simply to eat and keep a roof over one's head, philosophical questions about the meaning of life become luxuries indeed.

But gradually, as growing numbers of people's material standards of living increased, and day-to-day existence, at least in the West, became less arduous, these questions began to be asked by ever more people.

Relief from daily constant worry about providing the sheer necessities of life has been one overwhelming reason why more of us now have the freedom to live the lives that we want to live. But there are, I think, three other important strands which have come together to make the personal growth movement one of the biggest and most important of our times.

One is the demise of established, traditional religion. The second is the rise of psychoanalysis and the development of understanding about the conscious and unconscious mind. The third is the growth of mass education.

For the first time in history, large numbers of people have access to areas of information previously kept hidden, or limited to the privileged few. For example, until the beginning of this century, access to Buddhist, Hindu, and some other scriptures was available only to academics working in universities. There were no convenient translations available, and you could not go to a bookshop and buy a book on reincarnation, for instance.

The Demise of Established Religion

Until the beginning of this century, most people in the West unquestioningly accepted Christianity and its precepts. Although the original message of Christianity was one of peace, love and personal fulfilment, as time went on, religion had come to exert a repressive influence on people which made them live in fear of stepping out of line or asking awkward questions.

Organised religion came to back up and validate the class structure, the subordination of women, the inferiority of the lower orders and subject races. As ever more people started to question these concepts, religion began to lose its hold – and paved the way for a greater understanding of genuine spirituality.

The Rise of Psychoanalysis

In recent years there has been a lot of criticism of psychoanalysis, and detractors have argued that it tries to fit everybody into a sick society, rather than actually addressing the problems of the individual. But, whatever its drawbacks – and the fact that there are so very many different forms of therapy on offer indicates that nobody has yet got it exactly right – the rise of psychotherapy and psychoanalysis has had two immeasurable benefits: it helped to destroy the stranglehold of organised, repressive religion once and for all, and it helped society to realise that all of us, and not just the ruling classes, were equally important as human beings.

Before Freud, it had been assumed that most of us were probably 'normal', but that a few of us might be 'lunatics' and have to be locked up and forgotten about. One of the great contributions Freud made to modern thought was that *all* of us, whether we come from a royal palace or are born in a crumbling tenement, may be a mass of unresolved tensions and neuroses. None of us are 'simple', but all of us, whether educated and aristocratic or not, have an unconscious mind, which may be directing and influencing our actions in ways of which we are unaware.

Some people have called Freud the usher-in of a secular religion, and pointed out that his ideas of the id, the ego and the super-ego hark back to Old Testament ideas of sin and retribution. The significant difference was that God was now left out of the equation, and it was all down to us.

In the 1930s and 1940s, offshoots of Freudianism began to appear, and many of Freud's one-time disciples made their way to America, where they felt their ideas would perhaps fall on more fertile ground than had been the case in Europe. Many disciples went to California, where the human potential movement first began.

The ground-breaking aspect of this movement was that *everybody* had a right to fulfil their own potential, and realise who and what they truly were. We all had a right to be listened to, to be understood. And instead of looking outwards for satisfaction, we could look inwards instead. This was the movement which spawned the phrase 'navel-gazing', and like all pioneer movements, attracted a lot of suspicion and adverse comment in the early days.

From the start, the human potential movement attracted people who were interested in finding new ways of relating, new ways of living. It beckoned to those who were dissatisfied with society as it was, with its over-emphasis on material acquisitions, and who felt that life could be fuller, richer, more enjoyable and more meaningful through the process of self-discovery.

This movement quickly became known as the counter-culture, as its purpose was to spread peace and love, and to try and usher in a less materialistic, less acquisitive, patriarchal and hierarchical society.

Here are a few key people who helped to shape and organise this movement in its early days.

What is Personal Growth?

Wilhelm Reich, a clinical assistant of Freud's, was born in Austria in 1897. In 1939 he was forced to leave Austria because of his ideas, and also because he had become involved in Communism. He went to America, and there began the work for which he became most famous – that of discovering the source of the life energy, or orgone force, as he named it. Reich came to the conclusion that this force was powerfully released during orgasm, but at the same time it was a force, an energy which pervaded the whole universe. Orgasm was, as he saw it, a way of tapping into that energy, so that we could use it for our own self-development.

Reich placed enormous emphasis on the value of the orgasm in releasing pent-up feelings and inhibitions. He maintained that many of us try to protect ourselves from the vicissitudes of the world by building around ourselves a shell of 'body armour'. This works to protect and shield us in some ways, but it also prevents us from living and experiencing life to the full.

As physical tensions are gradually broken down, he believed, so the emotions can be released. Along with regular orgasms, massage and deep breathing can break down this shell which prevents us from attaining true self-knowledge, and also relating and connecting to other people. When we shut off, as so many of us do, we cannot ever have real empathy or relationships with others.

Reich pioneered what has come to be called bodywork, where the therapist actually touches the patient. Before this, the therapist had been hidden from the patient, sitting behind him or her as the patient lay down on a couch. There was no physical or even eye contact at all.

His ideas about the releasing and relaxing benefits of orgasm continue to attract, and the result of his work is a form of therapy known as Reichian bodywork. Release of pent-up emotions and long-buried traumas is encouraged by deep breathing and massage. This can result in screaming, spasms and tears as repressed emotions are remembered, relived and released.

Reichian therapy was extremely popular in America in the 1960s, and after a time in the doldrums, is now coming back into fashion. His lasting contribution to the personal growth movement, as I see it, is the importance he placed on releasing blocked emotions.

This, in fact, forms the cornerstone and starting point of any journey towards personal growth. Until blocked and negative emotions can be cleared, it is very difficult to proceed with any kind of 'enlightenment', as it is a bit like planting expensive seeds in poor soil which is covered in weeds. You first have to dig up the weeds, even if they have very long roots, and then fertilise the soil, before you can plant seeds of wisdom, fulfilment and positivity.

Another famous name from the early days of the human potential movement is that of *Werner Erhard*, who developed a form of therapy he called EST – Erhard Training Seminars. At these seminars, individuals in groups are led to a new awareness of themselves as the leaders try to help students break down their conventional images of themselves. EST began life in 1971, and the original seminars were sixty-hour courses lasting over two weeks, where students were not allowed to take breaks, had to surrender their watches, and 'break down' the old before the new could be built up.

EST, which is still going at Big Sur, California, where it all started, has changed and developed a lot since the early days, and it has certainly attracted much adverse comment. The organisation has now branched out into management training, self-improvement and 'prosperity' courses for businesspeople.

Perhaps one of the most influential people of all in the human potential movement was *Carl Rogers*, whose form of therapy has been taken on board by the burgeoning counselling movement, and who is seen as the father of much modern therapy.

Rogerian therapy differs from traditional therapy and forms of psychoanalysis in that it is client-centred. This means that the client and therapist are seen as equals, working together, rather than the therapist being the undoubted expert. In Rogerian therapy, the client is seen as his or her own greatest expert, with the therapist acting basically as a facilitator.

Carl Rogers put forward the idea that the basis for genuine therapy was unconditional love and acceptance, which means that the therapist does not judge the client, but helps him or her to see more clearly what is happening. Rogers also put great emphasis on empathy, by which he meant that the therapist should be able to enter into the world of the client, step into his or her shoes and see the world from the client's perspective, rather than imposing the therapist's own ideas. Rogers was one of the founders of humanistic psychology, and was influential in the development of present-day non-authoritarian therapies.

Another important name is that of *Abraham Maslow*, who formulated the idea of self-actualisation. According to Maslow, humans must first of all have their physical and survival needs met, such as those for food, shelter and sleep. When these are not a problem, we can start to fulfil our individual potential, and eventually 'actualise' ourselves (to realise the essence of ourselves, who we are as distinct from the roles we might play, such as mother, father, child, worker). Maslow was born in 1908, and his work differed from that of Freud and other early psychoanalysts in that he chose to concentrate on healthy, stable people rather than the obviously neurotic or disturbed.

Maslow was interested in what he termed 'peak experiences' which are moments of extreme joy and exhilaration experienced by people when they are well adjusted and emotionally healthy. Peak experiences have happened to all the great sages and founders of religion, Maslow said – but they can also happen to apparently ordinary people, once we have satisfied our other needs. After our basic needs have been met, we can then be ready to turn inwards and live our lives to the very fullest extent.

The work of these pioneer psychologists, plus the influence of mood-altering drugs and of Eastern religions, all came together in the 1960s to provide a very different outlook on life from anything which had happened before.

Basically, the new psychology movement stated that we are all important, we can all 'self-actualise', and that we all have the right to a happy, healthy, fulfilled life. Nobody need be left out.

In particular, the movement placed great emphasis on the spirit, the emotions, on what was going on inside, and gave us the chance to face up to ourselves, to discover what we really wanted and to make free, informed choices. It led to what has been derided as the 'me' generation, and its early adherents were accused of excessive narcissism, of thinking too much about themselves, rather than working towards a better society for everybody.

But what the human potential movement made clear from the very beginning was that it is impossible for society to change until individual members change first. Self-transformation, the movement maintained, must be the key to the transformation of society and the planet.

The Influence of Mass Education

Until the twentieth century, the great mass of people had been excluded from much knowledge and information. In many apparently civilised societies, from Ancient Greece onwards, only the well to do were allowed to learn to read and write, and have access to books. Slaves, serfs and very often women, even those from aristocratic backgrounds, were not given access to education, books or teachers. In the UK, people were burned at the stake for translating the Bible into English, so that it could be generally read, rather than its contents explained to the congregation by a priest.

In most Western countries, reformers had a hard time trying to make education available to the masses. One reason given was that if they were educated they could become discontent with their lot. And certainly, once people were allowed to learn to read and write, their discontent did grow. Because of this, the Trade Union Movement, the Workers' Educational Association and similar 'power to the people' organisations were formed.

Since those days, barriers have been breaking down all the time. But they have not completely gone, and many of us are relying too heavily on outside 'experts', rather than listening to our own voices. A genuine personal growth journey informs us that we can all be our own experts – and we need never rely on anybody else, or believe that they are better or more knowledgeable about ourselves than we are.

The Influence of Drugs

Up until the late 1950s and 1960s, very few people had ever taken mind-altering, or what came to be called psychedelic, drugs. They were confined to a few poets and seekers. Then, in the new freedoms that were felt in America in the 1950s, a whole generation of 'ordinary' people began to experiment with them.

The experiences of these people are chronicled in such books as Jack Kerouac's *On The Road*. Drugs seemed to open up new centres of the brain, and allow hitherto hidden perceptions and knowledge to be made manifest. For many people who tried them, drugs such as LSD appeared to open the gate to a whole new type of quasi-religious experience. In those days, it was known as 'blowing your mind'.

The trouble was, these drugs were always illegal – still are – and they led to chaotic lives, often resulting in imprisonment and early death for those who became gripped by their influence. Even so, they provided a glimpse for many into a world that appeared to be brighter, richer and less limiting than their ordinary, mundane existences.

We know now of the mental and physical damage that long-term drug-taking can do, and understand that it provides no real solution, no genuine path to enlightenment. But it was early experiments with drugs

such as LSD which allowed people to move out of their everyday existences, and glimpse something, however fleetingly, which was more
beautiful, more meaningful.

For some people, psychotropic drugs paved the way to a new consciousness. They played their important part in breaking down barriers,
opening up hitherto closed areas of the brain and enabling people to
realise that we are all, not just the geniuses and poets, highly complicated,
individuals with layers and layers of thought processes, emotions, perceptions and insights.

The New Centrality of Sex

People have always had sex, of course, but during the 1960s, sex came to
be seen in a different light – as something transcendental, mind-blowing
in itself, a way to gain important spiritual insights. Or at least, it could be.

This concept, of course, had its roots in Freudianism which maintained
that humans were above all, sexual beings, and that one of the reasons we
were unable to live life to the full was because our sexuality was repressed.
So much energy was taken up with containing and repressing our sexuality, according to Freud, that there was often little left over for anything
else of value.

If, he argued, we could all be gloriously sexually free and uninhibited,
then we would be able to know ourselves and become more genuinely
connected and intimate with others.

Wilhelm Reich (see page 13) was the main exponent of the notion that
full and free sexual expression, culminating in orgasm, was a potent way to
expand consciousness and relate to others in a loving, human, intimate
and uninhibited way. This movement was very popular from the start, and
resulted in what came to be called the 'permissive society', where sex
became elevated into a kind of religion of its own, with its own ritual and
complicated observances.

In America, swinging parties took place, and just about every kind of
sexual expression was allowed and encouraged. It was made possible of
course, by the invention of the pill. Previously, the fear of pregnancy had
been a potent reason for not wanting to get too heavily involved in sex.
Now, with this constraint removed, there was no longer any reason or
justification to say no . . .

This was the first time that free sexual expression had been allowed to

17

the masses. Previously, there had been small pockets of people who indulged in libertine practices, but it was all kept very quiet and secret. Now, for the first time, we could all harness and accept our sexuality.

Sex was seen as a way towards a new kind of intimacy, togetherness, commitment and mutual satisfaction. People began to see sex itself as spiritual, whereas previously, at least in the Christian tradition, it had been held as basically a sin, and a weakness for those who had not the 'gift of continency'. Sexual expression was now seen as a way to self-growth, a way of merging mind as well as body with another.

Free sexual expression reached its apotheosis in that most repressed of all countries, India, where the guru Bhagwan Shree Rajneesh held group sex sessions at his ashram in Poona.

The book, *The Joy of Sex*, written in two weeks flat by gerontologist Alex Comfort, himself no stranger to swinging parties, became a worldwide best-seller, and helped to start off an industry of sex manuals and videos which is still expanding.

Why did the Human Potential Movement start in America?

Although the seeds of the human potential movement were probably sown in Austria, they undoubtedly took root in America and not Europe. Why should this be?

American New Age writer Marilyn Ferguson, author of *The Aquarian Conspiracy*, says that Americans have been record-breakers and pioneers in every important modern field of endeavour, and have always exhibited greater self-reliance than other, older cultures. Ever since the founding fathers first landed in America in the early seventeenth century, the country has been seen as the place of freedom, the place where new ideas can flourish. America has always been far less hidebound than the old culture and the old order of Europe, she argues.

In America, there was no established class system, no 'pure' race, no ready-made culture – at least, not one that immigrant Europeans recognised. There was no tradition of feudalism and no idea that people ought to know their place and be content to stay in it.

At the same time, American culture has always had its repressive, guilt-ridden side. It was most likely the combination of being a new country where revolutionary ideas could flourish, plus the fact that so many Americans were chock-full of guilt feelings and inhibitions, which allowed the human potential movement to flourish, and eventually profoundly influence the world's thinking and attitudes.

America, Marilyn Ferguson reminds us, was the first country into the twentieth century, and it has always remained at the forefront of new ideas, in politics, science, psychology, literature, medicine and so on.

The Eastern Influence

At the same time as the human potential movement was gaining ground in California, a number of people, mainly young and middle class, were looking towards the East to find some kind of spirituality and meaning in life, which they felt was no longer present in the West.

At the same time, a number of Indian gurus and enlightened masters (many self-styled) travelled to the West in the 1960s to spread their message. Many of the Eastern-based spiritual movements which flooded into the West during the 1960s and 1970s tied up extremely closely with the human potential movement.

Until the end of the 1960s, very few people indeed in the West had any knowledge or information on the doctrines of reincarnation and karma, or the ideas of detachment and surrender. Eastern spiritual movements based on ancient Hinduism were instrumental in bringing these ideas to a mass audience, and they fitted in perfectly with the modern concepts of personal growth.

Put very simply, the doctrine of reincarnation, one of the most ancient belief systems in existence, holds that we all possess a non-physical element which does not perish like the body, but which goes on for ever, inhabiting new bodies when the old ones die. The doctrine of karma, inseparably linked with reincarnation, means that the kind of actions we perform in this life will affect the kind of birth we take next.

The practical implications of accepting these ideas mean that we will become far more responsible for our actions, because, in very direct ways, they will always rebound on us. And the more we 'grow', the more responsible and less blaming of others we will become.

The Eastern spiritual movements which have become popular since the 1960s came in to fill the gap left by the demise of established religion, and to meet the yearning that many of us have for some spiritual element in our lives. Genuine spirituality, as opposed to religion, means that we will always strive to be the very best of ourselves, we will take full responsibility for everything we do, we will do our best to overcome negative and self-sabotaging tendencies, we will try to see the best in others, and we will learn to love others properly – with detachment and respect, rather than trying to bind them to us.

Now, in place of prayer came meditation, the ability to still our minds and turn inwards. In place of dark-robed priests, vicars and ministers, came colourful gurus, with their chants, their mantras, their incense and their message of universal peace and love.

At first, there was a great deal of suspicion attaching to these gurus and their messages. But now, many of the concepts have been built into therapy, into medicine and into healing treatments of all kinds. The old and the new, modern science and exotic ancient practices came together to give a new world view, one which enabled us to see all of humanity as our brothers and sisters, to be separate and individual in ourselves, and yet to feel connected to other people, to our environment and to the planet.

The word 'spirituality' was initially regarded with great suspicion, so great was the backlash and intolerance of organised religion. But now, we can realise that the word need mean nothing more than a way of getting to know the essence of ourselves, the ability to strip away layers of negativity, conditioning and unhelpful habits of thinking, and allow the peaceful, positive, healthy and happy individual to shine through.

The first people to embrace the new spiritual message were those who felt they did not want to take on board the intensely materialistic lifestyle which had grown up since the Second World War. These were people who could perhaps afford to turn their backs on materialism as they had grown up in a world where nobody went hungry or poor. It is significant that it was in the world's richest country, America, that the hippy movement began.

Reviving Ancient Healing Arts

Barriers were falling down all over the place, as ancient and new met each other in the intense search for integrity, authenticity, individuality and health – a search which has been unique in the history of humankind because for the first time ordinary people, rather than just the educated upper classes, could take part.

What is Personal Growth?

The 1960s was the great age of medical science, of 'breakthroughs' and a pill for every ill. Many of us confidently believed that medical science had all but got illness zapped: it would be only a few years before there was a specific pill for every ailment which was liable to strike. Soon, it seemed, we would be able to take a pill that would make us slim, a pill that would cure cancer, a pill that would banish arthritis, a pill that would put an end to migraines.

After all, we already had a pill for the biggest problem that had previously confronted human relationships – that of unwanted pregnancy.

But, as we now know to our cost, things didn't turn out quite like that. Before long, we were realising that there was actually an ill *from* every pill. We also learned that pills didn't actually cure illnesses, but merely suppressed the symptoms, often allowing the underlying illness to get worse all the time. This is what happened with arthritis and the drug Opren. Also, it was found that most strong drugs had their adverse side-effects. And they didn't make us better at all.

As disillusion set in, people began to explore a new way of looking at health – the holistic way, which viewed people as mind, body and spirit working either in harmony or disharmony, each affecting the other. The old way had been to look at people as a collection of parts to be mended or cut out. You either put down the symptoms with a pill, or cut out the offending organ with surgery.

A few far-sighted doctors and health practitioners began to see this method of medicine as brutal, even anti-health, and started to promote 'gentle' methods – diet, exercise, spiritual healing, relaxation, meditation, visualisation – as effective ways of regaining health. Ancient methods of healing, such as astrology and herbalism, which had fallen into great disrepute since the rise of mechanistic medicine, began to be revived.

In the beginning, these 'gentle' methods were despised and rejected by the medical profession as unscientific and unproven. But gradually, they expanded into the mainstream and now very many orthodox doctors are learning homoeopathy, acupuncture, herbalism and hypnosis.

Gradually, the idea grew up that we could not rely on doctors or hospitals to nurse us back to health, but that basically we were all responsible for looking after ourselves and taking care of our own health. Many, if not most, of the ancient healing arts now being excitedly revived take as their axiom that all healing is ultimately self-healing, and that we can, if we are so minded, take steps to set this healing process in motion.

21

The Influence of Feminism

The current wave of feminism got off the ground in the early 1970s, when ever more 'ordinary' women began attending consciousness-raising groups, becoming 'sisters' and questioning what increasingly came to be seen as a patriarchal society which did not nurture women, but turned them into supporters and bolsterers of men and the male system.

Although there has, as many feminist historians have pointed out, been a women's movement throughout this century, this had previously confined itself to small pockets of protesters and radical thinkers. Even the British suffragette movement before the First World War was confined mainly to middle and upper-class women.

But now, women of all classes could liberate themselves. Or, at least, that was the message.

Hundreds of books about women's subjection to men poured out – again, most of the early and most radical ones came from America – and made thousands, perhaps millions of women who previously assumed they were happy with their lot, which they had chosen, think again. For many women, this kind of growth was painful indeed, as it made them confront the choices they had made within patriarchy.

The plight of women everywhere was echoed by that of the 'subject races'; and ever more people began to question the dominant white male system, seeing it as simply one way, and not the only, or necessarily the best, way to live and conduct ourselves.

The feminist ideas which seemed so revolutionary during the 1970s all accord perfectly with the personal growth movement. They reminded us that women could become sisters, supportive of each other, rather than being isolated and competing for the best males around. Women were encouraged to 'reclaim their power', which is what personal growth is all about.

At first, the radical feminist movement tended to be separatist, excluding men, and earned its adherents the label 'man-haters'. In fact, this was unfair as what the early feminists hated was not individual men, but the white male supremacist system, which they felt had destroyed women's integrity and individuality.

Into the Mainstream

The personal growth movement can no longer be ignored. Almost everybody has become touched by it in some way or other, even if there are still pockets of resistance. It has penetrated into offices and businesses, into medical science – ever more hospitals are treating chronically ill patients with massage, aromatherapy, relaxation and herbs – into family life, into the way we regard the environment.

After a few decades of intensely materialistic living, there is a deep and universal yearning for the spiritual, for the things which money cannot buy, such as peace of mind, physical and emotional health, good relationships, positive attitudes, for the things which are permanent and which cannot be snatched away from us.

As ever more aspects of modern life are crashing around us, such as traditional marriage, financial institutions, the property market – many of which previously seemed safe, solid and permanent – the yearning for inner peace and stability grows daily. It is being ever more widely appreciated that the only way to regain a sense of security is to be inwardly strong – and we must acknowledge that this may take some practice and hard work.

We now know that, when it comes down to it, the only people we can really rely on are ourselves. Our partners, parents, children, bosses, employees, may let us down. Our doctors, accountants, banks, lawyers, may not be acting in our best interests. Our jobs, houses, whole way of life, can go in an instant.

The only way to cope with sudden and sometimes frightening change in our lives is to acquire inner serenity. That is what personal growth means, and none of us can any longer afford to ignore taking its precepts on board if we want to be able to cope with whatever our life and circumstances may throw up.

The journey towards personal growth can help us to take charge of our circumstances at the same time as remaining flexible.

But how, with so many bewildering things on offer, from spiritual movements to therapy to healing treatments to retreats and growth centres, do you ever start to make the journey?

Read on – and all should become clear.

Chapter 2

Your Growth Journey

A successful growth journey is one that enables you to know yourself, to make authentic choices and to have a sense of purpose in life.

But how is it all to happen? How are we ever to know what we really want – and how can we hope to attain it?

The first thing to understand is that a journey towards personal growth will never place undue emphasis on the acquisition of material objects. This doesn't mean, however, that all of us engaged on the quest must give up our homes and jobs and comfortable lifestyles, and go and live like a hermit in a cave, renouncing possessions.

An important aspect of the journey is being able to look after ourselves, and provide adequately for our physical needs. There is nothing wrong in having a harmonious, well-furnished home, the very best food that you can get, and surrounding yourself with good music and good paintings and earning enough money to meet all your day-to-day needs. This ensures that you are not a drag on other people, or on the State, and that you can look after yourself. Self-reliance is an essential aspect of a growth journey. There should be no expectation that anybody else will ever provide for your needs, so the hope of a Prince Charming or an heiress suddenly arriving to take all your troubles away must be dismissed as illusion and fantasy.

Only you can provide for your needs – nobody else has any duty to provide for you, except of course, when you are a child and have no choice but to be dependent.

The main purpose of the quest is to develop those aspects of ourselves which enhance our own lives, and those of everybody we meet – the qualities of positivity, cheerfulness, self-respect, self-confidence and self-esteem – the qualities which impart internal strength and courage to face up to whatever might happen in the future, something none of us can ever predict or know about with any certainty.

When we continue to have over-attachment to material things, whether these are houses, jobs, relationships or even physical prowess, and we delight in these, we can never really get very far on the journey. The reason these should never be over-valued is because they can all – even wonderful physical health and strength – be snatched away in an instant.

John for instance, was a champion marathon runner. Every morning, he would go out for his jog, and he exulted in his extreme fitness. But one day, when he was jogging along as usual, he was hit by a car, and the impact was so great that bones from one shattered leg shot into the other.

It took John two years before he was even able to walk again. Now, he is not only walking again but running. But the steel pins in one leg continue to remind him that there was no security, no reliability, in his pursuit of fitness. In fact, it almost killed him.

One of the first and most important truths to be learned on a path of personal growth is that good health, good financial fortune, wonderful relationships or a super job may only be lent to us for a short time. Good health can disappear – eventually it inevitably will – so that although it is important to keep physically strong and fit, it must be remembered that nobody's good health lasts for ever, and frailty and old age will come to us all.

Good financial fortune is one of the easiest things to lose. Even money which seems to be extremely safely invested can be lost in spectacular crashes and depressions, and there is no guarantee that reverses won't happen to even the richest person. We see this happening all the time, as tycoons and businesses crash owing billions.

We are given to understand, by all the many books written on the subject, that it is important, even essential, to have good relationships, and in particular, a wonderful intimate relationship with one other person. When relationships are new, when there is wonderful sex, companionship and togetherness, this can sometimes feel like growth. Adrenaline can flow, and we can feel capable of anything. But the fact is that few intimate relationships stay wonderful for ever, and even the most transcendental sex with that person may well become boring and tedious eventually. There is also no certainty that any relationship, however close and supportive it seems, will last beyond tomorrow.

We have to realise that, although close, intimate relationships can appear comforting and life-enhancing, there is actually nobody outside ourselves who can ever give us happiness all the time. If we give other people that power, we have to realise that they have an equal ability to make us miserable. Only you can make yourself happy, by the attitudes you choose to adopt.

And only you can make the journey towards self-awareness, towards self-realisation. Nobody else can make the journey for you, because nobody else can *be* you.

But don't imagine that the journey will be a bleak one, with no money, no proper job, no satisfying intimate relationships or comforting friends. The good news is that if you embark on this path you will never actually want for money, friends or good relationships. As you become more positive, more serene, more self-confident and assertive, you will find that these things magically attach themselves to you. As you manage gradually to strip away the layers of negativity, you will find that good things come to you without you really seeming to try.

It is a universal law that whatever we give out, we get back. Increased self-confidence enables us to put a proper value on ourselves, not to take less than the going rate, and to be able to earn a good salary. Increased self-respect means that we will naturally live in a home that is welcoming and well looked after and be surrounded by objects which are both pleasurable and beautiful. There is nothing wrong with that. We deserve to have good quality in our lives.

And people who are positive, vibrant, smiling, happy and lively will attract similar kinds of people to themselves. If we feel lonely, we will attract another lonely person. If we are angry, we will attract angry people. If we feel ourselves to be victims, at the mercy of events, we will attract bullies and others who do us down.

A question people often ask is: what is the right age to begin a journey towards self-realisation? Should we start when we are young, wait until we are old, past retirement, or is it something that comes in as a solution to the mid-life crisis?

The short answer is that there is no ideal age, and it all depends on the individual. Some of us may feel ready in our teens, while for others it may not happen until we are in our fifties or sixties, or even older.

For many people, the starting point will be some kind of crisis in their lives – loss of a job, of a loved one, the end of a close relationship, a bout of serious ill-health. All these events can be seen as learning experiences, neither good or bad in themselves, but simply things that happen. What determines growth is how we manage to react to each crisis that crops up.

But don't imagine you have to wait for a severe crisis to begin your journey. Even simple curiosity, or a feeling that life could be richer and more fulfilling, may be enough to propel you towards taking the first steps.

Fears and Doubts

Some people may be afraid that embarking on the journey will mean that they lose all their individuality, and become indistinguishable from all the other happy, smiling, positive, cheerful people on similar journeys. Many people truly believe that their anger, aggression, short fuse and so on, is 'them' and if they lose these attributes, there will be nothing of 'them' left.

In fact, the exact opposite happens on a personal growth journey. It can be likened to polishing up a copper, pewter or silver object which has become tarnished and dull over the years. All you are doing when you are engaged on such a journey is bringing back the lustre, brilliance and individuality of yourself.

It is when we are covered in grime and dirt and negativity that we are exactly like all the other dirty, grimy objects. It's only when we polish ourselves up that our true self shines through.

But just as some objects need scouring with wire wool while others may simply need a polish with a soft cloth, so we all have different needs. This is why the journey has to be individual for each one of us. What works for one person may be quite wrong for another.

It is because of this that there are now so many organisations, treatments and therapies on offer. They have, in the main, developed out of dissatis-faction with what was already in existence, and made a wider choice available.

What works for you will be what accords with your inclinations, pocket, age group or needs at a particular time. However, for everybody who attempts the journey, there must be some attention paid to these vital aspects:

- fulfilling your own potential
- excising negative thoughts (about yourself and others)
- letting go of stress and tension
- becoming aware of intuition

- letting go of fear
- becoming more loving
- getting to know yourself
- making informed choices
- staying physically well and healthy
- not being a victim
- following your own path
- being alive to new ideas
- staying young in outlook
- increasing your intelligence
- freeing yourself from addictions
- clearing blocked emotions
- choosing a good diet
- having good relationships
- feeling connected to others
- having awareness of planetary needs

I'll look at these aspects briefly now, one by one.

Fulfilling Your Own Potential

This means that you should not try to help other people fulfil their potential, but concentrate on yourself. Parents should, of course, make sure that their children have everything they need to maximise their own abilities – that's what being a good parent is all about. But none of us needs to be a parent to another adult human being, and neither should children be seen as people who will fulfil the untapped potential of their parents.

We cannot realise anybody else's ambitions, nor can they realise ours – fulfilling potential is a search which must be wholly and fully individual.

It has been estimated by child psychologists that most children use, at most, 10 per cent of their potential. By the time they reach adulthood, they are likely to use even less. But it should not be imagined that if we used all of what we have inside us, that we would all become geniuses, any more than a daisy can ever become an orchid.

Some of us will always be daisies, while others will be exotic orchids – but we can all learn to flower to the best of our ability.

The fact is that all too many of us give up at an early age and don't even use the talents that we have, or used to have. This happens partly because of fear, because of a terror of trying and being found wanting, or being rejected, and partly (at least for some of us) because it appears to be better, more worthy, to forget about our own ambitions and 'devote' ourselves to other people.

Women have been particularly adept at this, cheerfully giving up 'promising' careers as writers, painters, musicians or whatever to 'devote' themselves to a man, to their family or some other person. Then, before they know what is happening, that wonderful talent has disappeared.

The reasons why so many of us fail to fulfil our individual potential are complex. One is ego. We can be so frightened and nervous at the thought of failure that this will be enough to stop us even from trying. So, in order not to have to come to terms with what we imagine are the limitations of our own talents and abilities, we put handicaps on ourselves, sabotage ourselves, tell ourselves we can't. It is so common for us to sabotage ourselves that half the time we are not even aware that we might be doing it.

Other reasons for not making the best of ourselves are fear, lack of self-confidence, a misplaced idea of duty towards others, and a childhood history of being put down by parents and teachers – very common, and sometimes difficult to overcome in adult life. By no means all families and parents are supportive or nurturing, and it can be painful to realise and admit this is your experience.

An important aspect of personal growth is that it enables us to access and address the areas of self-sabotage – whatever the reasons for this – so that we no longer continue to limit ourselves. Anger, aggression, flying off the handle, feeling resentment; all ways in which all too many of us may limit and short-change ourselves.

When we are able to harness the ability to fulfil our potential, we have the confidence to be able to fail or, at least, not necessarily to attain every time the high standards we may have set ourselves in our heads. But the only way to become a great composer, pianist or artist is simply to keep doing it, work through the difficulties, the doubts, the uncertainties. The more world-class any artist is, the more they practise and keep on trying to improve their art.

It is commonly assumed that if you have a particular talent, then this will come out of its own accord. But it is not necessarily the case. You may be denying and minimising your talents because you are afraid of what might happen if you try to tap them. And it's never too late. For example

Julia Margaret Cameron the pioneer photographer, didn't pick up a camera until she was 48 and the late Jane Ewart-Biggs became a confident speaker in the House of Lords only after her husband was assassinated.

You may not be able to realise your potential until you are able to have some space to yourself to think, meditate, relax. If you try to empty your mind, it will probably come to you sooner or later what you are meant to do. And if ever an idea surfaces, however fantastic it may be, don't dismiss it instantly, but stay with it for a while, and see whether it develops into anything. Fulfilling potential means always to be alive to the possibility of change and a new direction.

There are now many growth organisations and movements which are designed to help you activate and tap your particular talents and abilities. It may be that you will need help to uncover your real purpose in life.

Excising Negative Thoughts

This one is not as easy as it sounds, and may not be achievable by a simple act of will. Over the years, most of us have, usually without realising it, got into the habit of being negative, resentful, hostile, fearful, envious and nervous – without fully appreciating that these *are* negative ways of thinking.

We can also so easily limit ourselves by telling ourselves that we can't do certain things. These are limits that do not need to be there. We may have been told in our youth that we were clumsy, inept, surly, highly-strung – and we have now come to believe these pronouncements. We may also see ourselves as short-tempered, easily angered, unable to suffer fools gladly. Again, these will often be things we have been told about ourselves by others.

When we accept negative messages about ourselves, we will inevitably believe similar things about other people as well. Because holes have been picked in what we were trying to do, we will try to denigrate other people's achievements and attainments too. Instead of sharing in their success, delighting in the fact that they may have been successful in one way or another, we will try to run them down.

We all do it to some extent, but the important thing to realise is that when we run other people down, we run ourselves down, instead of bolstering ourselves up.

But once we can start to see the positive side of what others are doing – and it does take practice and vigilance – we can then start to feel more at ease with ourselves, less threatened, less fearful. Extremely negative people, those who seem to hate and despise everybody else, are really those lacking in true self-esteem. Such people inwardly hate themselves, and they are projecting this hatred outwards. Don't be influenced by them, or imagine that it's clever to hate and resent – it's just the opposite.

Some people may think that if they criticise and condemn all the time, this means they are exercising true judgement. In fact, it merely tells us that they are highly negative people we would do well to avoid. Who wants to be in the company of a person who is constantly running everybody else down?

It is not always easy to learn to love yourself, but taking part in the growth activities described in this book, where you are able to concentrate entirely on yourself, will help you to recognise and strip away the layers of negativity that may have accumulated over the years, to reveal the genuine positivity underneath.

It is most often the case that those who virulently run down others have been hurt and harmed themselves, usually in their early years. They may need to release that long-held hurt from their system before any meaningful journey can begin. There are now effective ways of discharging and releasing old hurts from the system so that they no longer have any power over us (see pages 104–106).

But often, just the realisation that it does nobody any good to hate can, in itself, open up the way to significant personal growth. If you try to see the positive qualities of other people rather than their negative sides, the world will gradually become a rosier, less hostile and more welcoming place. When we hate, we fear – and fear is inimicable to genuine personal growth.

Letting Go of Stress and Tension

Like negative thoughts, holding stress and tension in the system can become ingrained habits. Over a period of time, we may get so used to our stress that we no longer notice it any more, but just imagine that's how we are – chronically tired and tense.

Most of us will be holding at least a certain amount of stress in our body, and it makes sense to embark on a specific programme to release this, as it's not doing any good at all.

31

There is now a wide variety of therapies, such as massage, aromatherapy, meditation, autogenic training and the Alexander Technique, all of which can help to release ingrained stress. As it can be difficult to be at peace with yourself when there is chronic stress in the system, making the decision to rid yourself of excess tension can be a useful first step on the path to growth – rather like priming a door before painting it.

Gentle physical therapies can help to put you back in touch with your body, which you may have ignored and ill-treated for years, and help you to realise just where the stresses and strains are. Never feel that such 'pampering' of yourself is a waste of time and money. The more attention of this kind you can give to yourself, the more functional you will be able to become, both for yourself and in your relationships with other people. Releasing stress from the system also allows more energy to become available for other, worthwhile things that you may want to pursue.

Becoming Aware of Intuition

In our present Western society, we have come to overvalue logic and reason, and have tended to forget that there are valuable ways of gaining knowledge and information other than through conscious, apparently rational thought processes. The creative flash and the instinct that tells us we should or should not be doing something, has tended to become overridden with our modern insistence that the scientific method is more valid, more accurate.

It takes practice for most of us to learn to listen to our intuition, as we may well have forgotten how to rely on it, or call it into being. But what the personal growth journey achieves more than anything else is to enable us to trust what is coming from our own inner voice, our gut feeling, and then to bring the reasoning process in to check this out. When we learn to trust our intuition, this means we remember how to feel, rather than just how to think. We need to have both the rational and the intuitive, both the left and the right brain methods of gaining information, but in the recent past, intuition has been derided as something belonging to women – and therefore seen as inferior and able to be disregarded.

Letting Go of Fear

Many of us allow ourselves to be completely hemmed in by needless fears. We may be afraid of growing old, afraid that our partners will leave us for somebody younger, more attractive or richer, afraid that we may lose our jobs, that our houses will be burgled. We are afraid of travelling in case we are mugged or raped, afraid of talking to strangers at parties in case we are rebuffed. We are afraid of being assertive, of asking for what we want, and afraid of acknowledging our own needs or making sure that they are met.

We may be afraid to speak in public, of singing in public, afraid of making fools of ourselves in all kinds of ways, afraid we will fail, afraid of what other people might think of us.

However can we hope to get rid of all these fears, which affect every aspect of our daily lives?

A big step on the way is realising that, in fact, we have nothing whatever to fear. Although in some ways, fear may seem to be a useful survival mechanism, many of us have got used to fearing things which are simply not inherently frightening. The other thing to remember about fear is that fearing something won't prevent it from happening, and may even help to bring it about. For instance, if we fear that our partner may leave us, this may make us act in all kinds of controlling ways to try to make them stay, so that eventually the other person is exasperated into leaving.

If we fear that our children may get run over on the roads, we may not instil self-confidence and self-reliance into them, so that they become able to take care of themselves. If they remain frightened every time they cross the road, they will be hesitant – and so that much more likely to have an accident.

When we continue to fear things that are not inherently dangerous, we restrict our lives and our experiences. But for most of us, living with fear has become such a habit that it often seems easier not to face up to it. But this is the first thing you have to do in order to grow.

Psychologist Susan Jeffers, whose book *Feel the Fear and Do it Anyway* (Century) has helped a lot of people to overcome their fears, says that people in the public eye, those who seem so very confident, aren't people who don't have any fears, but those who have managed not to let them stand in the way of what they want to do. Most artists and creative people have terrible fears all the time when they are faced with a blank canvas or sheet of paper – yet they don't let these fears stop them from writing down some words, or making marks on the canvas.

Every time we face up to a fear, however minor this may seem to others, we score a victory and increase our self-confidence. But, when we let fears dominate our lives, we never get to know ourselves properly, as the fears actually block out self-knowledge. Most of all, when we fear, we are afraid to get to know ourselves properly, in case we don't like what we find.

The truth is that when we allow ourselves to start facing up to what we have come to fear, we will discover that we are cleverer, more talented, more creative – not less – than we ever imagined.

Becoming More Loving

This is really the essence and heart of personal growth. It is all about discovering love – proper love that is – rather than romance, eroticism, sex or trying to bind other people to us permanently. All these are false expressions of love. But as humans, love is our very deepest need, and most of us do what we do because we want to be loved, however perverse this may seem to others.

When we can learn to love and accept ourselves, we can then learn to love other people properly, and see them not just in relation to ourselves, but as they truly are. It is love which enables genuine spiritual healers to do their work; love which makes what we call extra-sensory perception possible.

But like any other important skill, loving oneself and other people often has to be learned, because we have forgotten, or perhaps never known, how to do it. Loving oneself and others comes with increased self-confidence and self-esteem, and also a diminution of negative qualities such as greed and ego.

Getting to Know Yourself

The ability to face up to ourselves is the greatest test of a personal growth journey. It means, above all, being able to separate who and what we are from the roles we may be playing at any particular time. We may be acting as mothers, fathers, employees, employers, children, wives, husbands – but these roles are not *us* – they are only how we may be seen by certain significant other people.

Some people are terrified of losing their roles, so closely have they identified with them. A woman who has put everything into being a mother, for instance, may be terrified at the thought that one day her children may leave home and not need her any more. A politician may find it hard to cope with life when he or she is no longer elected; a doctor may wonder what on earth to do in retirement. It is important to realise that these roles, or any others that we might play, are not the whole of what we are, even though of course they may be an important aspect.

The journey towards getting to know ourselves may involve pain, as we have most probably denied and minimised important aspects of ourselves over the years. We may have no idea of what we are really like, especially if we have simply accepted other people's valuations of us.

Making Informed Choices

This means getting to know all the pros and cons before setting out on a course of action, rather than just hoping against hope that things will turn out for the best. As with other aspects of living life to the full, it sometimes takes courage to get to know all the ins and outs, rather than just stumbling from one thing to the next.

The ability to make informed choices involves asking ourselves what we really want out of life – in itself often a very difficult question to answer – how we might be able to achieve it, and how our choices may affect other people. It also involves accepting responsibility for whatever consequences might ensue.

If we tell ourselves that we are doing the best we can, having fully investigated all the options available, then we need never reproach ourselves or, what is possibly worse, blame other people for the choices we may have made.

People who say 'I did it because of you' are unfairly foisting responsibility for their choices on to others, and evading personal responsibility.

We have to realise that we, and we alone, are responsible for the choices we may have made, and act accordingly. It serves no purpose to blame others, or even 'society' for what we may have done in the past. When we blame other people, we make ourselves powerless victims, and imagine that nothing can ever be done to make matters right.

It is true that we may have been given, or acted on, wrong information – but the people giving us that information knew no better. If they could have put us right, they would have.

Staying Physically Well and Healthy

This is also very much a choice. Although we are born with different constitutions, and some of us are more robust than others, we can, if we like, make the choice to be well or, conversely, to be ill.

Of course, heredity and environmental factors play their part, but we are not entirely at the mercy of our genes or environment. If we sincerely want to stay well, we will make sure we avoid build-up of stress, give ourselves the best possible diet and pace ourselves properly.

It is becoming increasingly clear that a major factor in ill-health is stress, which results in our immune systems becoming less efficient or, under severe and prolonged stress, perhaps packing up altogether, as happens with AIDS patients. In fact, there is growing evidence to suggest that AIDS is, above all, a disease of fear. When patients have AIDS, or are HIV diagnosed, they feel they are under a death sentence, and the enormous fear this imposes causes their immune systems to become ever less efficient.

In order to stay well, it is important to make sure we do not abuse our bodies in ways that cause their workings to be less efficient, and to be cheerful all the time. Cheerfulness and positivity, plus lack of resentment and anger, make for lasting physical good health.

Getting to know our bodies and how they work is an important aspect of personal transformation. It's not enough to live in one's head, or even one's heart. We are all housed in bodies, and mind, body and spirit are intimately interlinked, not separately-operating units.

It is a sign of self-respect to be able to look after ourselves physically. It means we are honouring the physical vehicle in which we find ourselves.

Not Being a Victim

Being a victim means to be powerless. When we are, or feel ourselves to be, powerless, we tend to blame other people for our present circumstances and never look to ourselves. We may come to feel that we can never lift ourselves up, never take charge, until 'they' do something. We stop being victims when we begin to realise that we can always do things for ourselves, here and now. We don't ever have to wait for anybody else to make things all right for us – at least, not once we become adult.

The word 'victim' is very much used nowadays to denote those who have suffered incest, other forms of abuse, battered women, those who have been on the receiving end of a burglary or break-in, and those who have been hostages, or imprisoned in terrible conditions in foreign countries.

When you are a victim, you are on the receiving end of other people's cruel actions, and may feel there is nothing whatever you can do about it. But to inculcate the victim mentality makes us ever weaker, and more prone to be victims in every aspect of our lives.

Victims wait for things to happen to them, rather than trying to take charge of their circumstances. So, the first step in not being a victim is not to see yourself as one, but to view yourself as powerful and strong. Even if you have been abused as a child – and many of us have, in one way or another; if not physically or sexually, then by having our self-confidence destroyed, being emotionally blackmailed, forced into professions or marriages to please our families and so on – this doesn't mean you have to be a victim for life.

Usually, the first step in not being a victim is to try to get to the bottom of what caused this attitude in the first place. In many cases, it will have been set in motion by childhood events. We have to realise that although we may have been victims then, we don't have to be now – it needn't be a life sentence.

As an adult, nobody needs to be a victim. Many women feel they are victims of the men in their lives, and men often feel victims of 'the system', of their bosses or lack of education, but extricating oneself from victimhood is always possible.

You cannot both take charge of your life and remain a victim: the two are mutually exclusive. Taking charge of your life doesn't mean that terrible things will never happen again; there is nothing you can do to guarantee against this. Burglaries, redundancies, accidents, reversals of fortune – any of these may still happen. The difference is that when you no longer have a victim attitude, you will not be devastated by such events.

The journey of personal growth can show us how to stop being a victim, how to take charge, and what is the difference between the two.

Following Your Own Path

We all live in societies where certain types of behaviour are encouraged, whereas others are frowned on. The great majority of us follow the prevailing orthodoxy, without ever asking ourselves whether this choice might actually be right for us. One of the main criticisms of psychiatry and psychoanalysis is that it tries to fit people into a sick society, rather than ever asking whether it's our present values that are wrong rather than people's ability to fit in with them.

For instance, very many people imagine that at some stage in their lives, they 'have' to get married and become parents. Most of us don't appreciate that we have an equal choice *not* to do these things, and that this can be equally, perhaps even more, valid.

Certain types of behaviour are labelled 'normal' and others, 'deviant'. Although there are, of course, certain behaviours that anybody would consider deviant and unacceptable, there is no reason why we should all feel we have to fit in with what is currently considered 'normal'.

For example, writer Quentin Crisp dyed his hair, minced along the streets, and wore nail varnish and lipstick as a young man in the 1930s so that nobody would be in any doubt as to what he was – an effeminate homosexual. He lives his own life and does his own thing completely – which is one reason why, in spite of never having proper jobs or a proper income, and living in the same filthy room for over 30 years, he is still hale and hearty at over 80. Most people would not have his courage or, perhaps, they would not realise with such clarity what they were.

The personal growth journey helps us to uncover our own paths, when these might have been obscured by inappropriate ideas of what is right and proper – and to have the courage to face up to what we are. It also helps us to understand that when we follow a path that is not really us, we harm ourselves and others. We can learn to be authentic – and worry less about what other people might think of our choices.

Being Alive to New Ideas

This is the realisation that nothing is set in concrete, and that most of our present knowledge is an interim statement only, which will do until we have more information, or until more light is shed on the subject. Think how many scientific 'certainties' have been overthrown over the years: there is no reason to believe this won't continue to happen.

All too often, we try to limit our horizons by believing that now we know all there is to know on a certain subject and therefore we can close the book. But so often, our beliefs and supposed knowledge are not the result of careful investigation into the subject, but the result of ignorance, prejudice and laziness.

In our non-growth mode, new ideas can seem threatening, disruptive and the old ones safe, simply because we are used to them. But when we gain self-awareness and self-confidence, we can take new ideas on board and be ready to throw out the old ones, or to look at them from a different perspective. We need no longer worry about what other people might think, or whether we might be considered odd to hold ideas which go contrary to accepted orthodoxy on a given subject.

When we gain the confidence to explore new ideas, we can feel we are reaching our own conclusions, rather than being told what to think, and just accepting the status quo.

Staying Young in Outlook

This means being aware that the soul, or spirit, unlike the body, is ageless, and does not deteriorate as the years go by. We can see visibly the ageing of the body, and imagine that *we* are getting old. But, in terms of personal growth and spiritual awareness, this is not the case.

It is only the physical vehicle, the car, if you like, which gets old and eventually has to be replaced. But we, who are the drivers, don't necessarily have to be replaced at the same time.

If we can realise that the motive force within us, which is not physical and which has no dimensions, cannot age, then we will inevitably stay young in our outlook. We will realise that there is no need to become crabbed, bitter and disillusioned with age, or have a closed mind. We do not need to shut ourselves off from new experiences. The soul is never tired, and never sleeps. There is no reason why our ideas should solidify and harden, along with our arteries. Staying young in outlook means to remain enthusiastic, hopeful, lively and positive – whatever the calendar might say.

Increasing Your Intelligence

It's often assumed that intelligence is a fixed quantity, something given at birth and for ever after unalterable, like the colour of our eyes or our genes. This is not the case. Almost all of us can increase our intelligence by making sure the mind always has something new to chew on, and that we are not letting bitterness and anger cloud our judgement.

Many of us limit our intelligence by telling ourselves we can't do this or that, that we are 'no good' with computers, or 'can't understand' numbers. In this way, we risk giving away our power to other people, by imagining they must be far cleverer than we are. But although clearly there are great differences in talent and ability, most of us can learn the simple survival skills of balancing a cheque book, driving a car, cooking a meal or making pleasant conversation.

When we tell ourselves that we can't do certain things, we are putting brakes on our intelligence and experience. It's also the case that when we can separate ourselves from our negative thoughts – anger, bitterness, guilt and worry – we can increase our intelligence and perceptions significantly. Intelligence also increases when we can separate ourselves from our addictions, as these cloud judgement and discrimination. We can separate ourselves from our addictions by understanding what is 'us' and what are addictions. For instance, many people believe they are angry, hostile, resentful people, whereas in fact, they are exhibiting learned, addictive behaviour.

Basically, high intelligence means having the ability to make connections, be able to concentrate and have powers of discrimination. All these can be increased or decreased, by our attitudes and view of ourselves, as time goes on.

Clearing Blocked Emotions

This is most important. One problem is that we don't always know whether we've got blocked emotions, or what these might be, because we have repressed and consciously forgotten them over the years.

Some personal growth organisations hold the view that if you practise conscious positive thinking, all old, inappropriate negative habits and emotions will eventually die away. My own view is that they often go too deep for this, and may have to be relived and released before their baleful hold can be relinquished. Sometimes, this can be like mining for diamonds.

In some cases, it may be necessary to have professional help for clearing blocked emotions. Otherwise, we may remain stuck in certain situations and attitudes which mean we can't advance, but go round in the same groove all the time.

There are now several highly effective techniques available for clearing old repressed emotions from the past. These are described in greater detail in the *Healing Treatments* section of the book and, for many people, they will be a powerful route to the journey of self-transformation.

Choosing a Good Diet

This may perhaps seem a trivial concern but if you think about it, all religions and spiritual paths have put dietary restrictions on their adherents. One of the reasons for this is to increase awareness that certain kinds of food and drink can affect both the body and the mind. Some foods help to promote insights, according to ancient doctrines. These are the natural, unprocessed foods which the body accepts and digests easily such as fresh, organic vegetables, whole wheat products, unprocessed nuts and whole grains.

Others stimulate the senses and may be aphrodisiac as well. They are the highly spiced and strong-tasting foods. Then, lastly, there are the foods which make us feel dead inside – the processed, denatured, lifeless foods and drinks, such as coffee, alcohol, highly sugared and coloured food and drink.

In order to facilitate our journey, we should try to choose foods that are fresh, not too stimulating, and not addictive or mood-altering. These are the foods which help rather than hinder mental awareness.

Having Good Relationships

Hundreds of books have been written, most of them since the 1950s, on how to have good relationships. Most of these books concentrate on intimate one-to-one heterosexual relationships. But, really, the whole subject is much wider than this.

We should have the aim of having good relationships with everybody we meet, realising that some will be casual and temporary, while others may become intimate, close and long-lasting.

When we feel at peace and harmony with ourselves, we will automatically start to have better relationships with other people. We will become less bitter, less resentful and envious, and realise that when we feel good about ourselves, we will feel better about others.

Looking for other people's positive qualities and concentrating on these rather than enlarging their faults enables us to improve our vision of ourselves.

Feeling Connected to Others

When we can increase our self-awareness, we will begin to have a sense of connectedness not only to other people, but also to all living things. We will not want to harm anybody or anything, understanding that when we do we harm ourselves, because we destroy our own compassion.

A sense of connectedness is what lies behind all good, genuine, intimate relationships. We begin to have empathy with others, we start to be able to see things from their point of view, and no longer try to dragoon everybody into thinking as we do.

When we feel connected, this also means we maintain a definite sense of our own and other people's boundaries. We realise the separateness of others, as well as their connectedness. The difference between healthy and unhealthy relationships is that with the latter, we have no real idea where we might end and they begin. This means that we can treat them as extensions of ourselves, without respect, without any sense that they may have feelings of their own which we don't share.

Parents and children, and husbands and wives commonly have no sense of boundaries, of what is appropriate, and no idea how to respect each other as individuals. It is when boundaries become blurred that people can commit incest and other atrocities on others.

The whole notion of codependency, the state of being over-dependent on and addicted to other people, is based on this enmeshed idea of relationships. The paradox is that when we can become aware of clear boundaries, we can become more connected to others. When we are in touch with our own feelings, we are more likely to be in touch with other people's.

Having Awareness of Planetary Needs

This also springs out of feeling connected and in harmony with nature – an extension of feeling in harmony with ourselves.

42

We can only ever feel connected to other living, and even non-living, things when all the aspects of ourselves – mind, body and spirit – are integrated together. When we can come to feel this – and often it takes considerable work to arrive at this stage – we can feel the whole world operates according to universal laws, that things are not random and chaotic.

When this happens, we are much less likely to want to throw a spanner in the works, to try to impose control where this is patently impossible. We become instead far more interested in preservation and conservation, realising that it is actually impossible for us to impose our wills on nature for very long.

For very many people, a growing self-awareness automatically leads to planetary awareness, the realisation that we are part of the cycle of nature, not separate from it, and not superior to it. Ecological considerations have always been a close concern of those interested in their own personal growth.

Starting the Journey

If you wander round an event such as the Festival of Mind, Body and Spirit, held in London every May, you may well feel bewildered. There are so many things on offer – how do you ever start to look for the right one, the one most suitable for you?

All the stands, the seminars, the workshops, seem to be offering the same thing – the chance for personal transformation. Surely they can't all work?

And how do you know whether they are all genuine? Well, you can't be absolutely certain. But if you approach the whole thing with cynicism and suspicion, you are never likely to make the first step.

Some people assume that all New Age artefacts such as crystals, tarot cards, essential oils and aura healing, must be a load of rubbish and hokum, and leave it there. The point is that none of these has any inherent magic, but may or may not be ways in for some people, to the journey.

A rule of thumb is that if you like the sound of something or somebody, go with your intuition and see where it leads you – so long as it does not commit you to spending large sums of money, or embarking on a three-year course that it may be difficult to get out of. The more you investigate with an open mind, the sharper will become your antennae. It is not always helpful to go on personal recommendation, as what suits one person may be quite wrong for another. So, try to make up your own mind.

But if you get strong gut feelings, either pro or anti, have the confidence to go with these. Very often, people are drawn into what they need for a particular time; then the need may vanish, and something else present itself.

Some people are afraid of becoming New Age junkies, trying one thing after another, and never really getting anywhere, never arriving at any genuine enlightenment. But there is no real harm in this, so long as the movements and groups themselves are not harmful or exploitative.

Will My Journey Affect Others?

The answer to this question is undoubtedly yes. Nobody can both grow and stand still, so inevitably all your relationships with other people are going to be affected in some way.

The most problematic areas are usually with your intimate relationships, with family and close friends. It may be that your partner does not want you to 'grow', as he or she has got used to you as you are. When you embark on a journey like this, you will undoubtedly become a different person. You will gain new insights, new information about yourself and gradually you will start to see everything in a new light, with a different pair of specs.

It is true to say that nothing will ever seem the same again. You will have a potent feeling of scales falling from your eyes, and awareness that you can now see things that were formerly hidden.

There may be enormous fear on the part of other people in your life that, because of the journey you are undertaking, you will grow apart, see things in your partner or friends that were not apparent before, and which may not be so pleasing with the new vision.

Usually, you will want to take your partner with you on the journey, but this will often be highly resisted. Only you can decide how far to go and how much your personal journey is worth the cost of possibly losing previous close relationships.

Sometimes it may happen that one or other of you will meet a new person along the path, somebody who more closely shares your new way of living and thinking. Naturally, the partner left behind will not like this.

Partners who themselves do not want to grow, or who are not ready to start their own journey, will often like to believe that their loved one is being brainwashed by a dangerous cult, or that they have lost their marbles. They may make strenuous efforts to persuade them not to continue the journey.

The realisation that your partner, family or spouse may have a vested interest in keeping you as you were can be one of the most painful things to accept about a growth journey. One might imagine that family and friends will always want the best for you, but sadly this is not always the case.

If a relationship cannot take the strain of a growth journey, then it will have to be reassessed and re-evaluated. It may be that it has become unhealthy and dysfunctional, controlling or addictive, and that you will see this in the light of your new experience. When you embark on a growth journey, every aspect of your life and thought will eventually come under the microscope, for that is the nature of the quest.

The best that can happen is that in an intimate relationship, both of you will be able to benefit from the insights gained from the personal development of one partner. But this cannot be guaranteed.

Partners often tend to want to cling on to what they know, and prefer to stay in the cage rather than take the risk of flying into freedom. Because of this, it can happen that relationships will break up. If they do, then they were probably at the end of their life anyway. It is not always a sad thing to end a relationship – sometimes you just have to move on. And a relationship which has come to an end has not necessarily failed, but lived out its natural life.

There is no particular virtue in continuing relationships which have long become dead and meaningless. It frequently happens anyway that a growth journey is begun out of intense dissatisfaction with the status quo.

But before starting out on your journey you may have to ask yourself whether you would be prepared for this to happen. It is well known that the families of alcoholics and other addicts, for instance, often do all they can to keep the alcoholic dependent on his drink, even while strenuously denying they are doing this.

A wife or husband may say, and strongly believe, that they want the alcoholic to recover and become sober. Yet recent research into alcoholics and their families has shown that, more often than not, partners form alliances with alcoholics simply *because* they are addicted and dependent. If the alcoholic recovers, the partner may lose his or her role.

Similarly, a man may have married a much younger, less well educated and extremely dependent wife. This scenario is so common that it seems a normal, average situation. Yet, as time goes on, the wife may start to assert herself, go to consciousness-raising classes, become a feminist, get a job, get a degree. She is no longer so childlike, so dependent – and the relationship will inevitably change. The formerly dependent wife may have her eyes opened to what her husband is really like, and may come to see him as a bully, and not very intelligent or superior at all.

Sometimes we have to face the fact that it's time to let old relationships die and new ones come into being. This does not mean that there should be regret or recrimination: simply that one aspect of growth – learning from the past – has now been completed and a new phase must begin.

In the early stages, you may feel you are losing all your previous support networks, or come to the conclusion that these networks weren't as supportive as perhaps they appeared. Of course, this does not mean you have to abandon your responsibilities and simply walk out of a situation you no longer like. Genuine growth journeys are not about escape, but facing up to everything about your life – your past, your present, your future – and putting yourself in charge of all aspects of it.

PART 2
THE ENTRIES

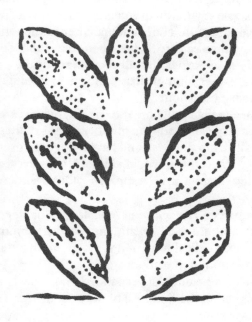

There are many routes and paths to self-transformation, although all will be aiming at the same goal – the emergence of the true, loving, positive person that may have been hidden behind a mass of negativities, wrong assumptions, lack of self-confidence and self-respect, and fears and doubts.

At first, it may all appear to be a complete jungle, bewildering in the extreme. In order to provide some kind of path and guide, I have divided the various aspects into relevant chapters.

There are a number of *personal growth organisations* (Chapter 3) which run seminars, workshops, conferences, either on a residential or day basis, for those who wish to explore particular areas further, or to try and become more effective in their everyday lives.

These organisations almost always have a founder, somebody usually with a personal vision, who has been able to put his or her ideas across to a wider audience. Many are extremely well established now and highly regarded, even though some were considered cranky and strange at first.

After the organisations come the *self-help groups* (Chapter 4). Many of these are for people trying to overcome addictions of various kinds – alcoholism, drug addiction, codependency, sex addiction – or perhaps a serious illness, such as cancer. It has been found that self-help groups, where everybody is as 'expert' as all the others in the group, are more effective than any other kind of therapy for people caught up in various kinds of compulsive behaviour.

After the self-help groups, come the *spiritual movements* (Chapter 5), of which there are a large and growing number. Many of these, although not all, come originally from the East, and have helped thousands of people to access and understand the spiritual side of themselves, without getting caught up in the dogma and trappings of conventional, established religions.

The final group of entries is *healing treatments* (Chapter 6) – alternatives to conventional and medical treatment. People commonly seek out healing, rather than medical treatments, when they have a chronic illness which has not responded to orthodox care.

The whole field of healing has expanded enormously in recent years, and is getting bigger all the time. All of the healing treatments described in this section work on the triple levels of mind, body and spirit, and provide healing for the whole person. There is never any guarantee that they can make you better, any more than there is with orthodox treatments, but they will at least help to further your self-knowledge and understanding, which is essential for continuing physical, emotional and mental health.

For large numbers of people, the route towards self-transformation lies in coming to terms with serious illness. It is becoming increasingly evident that people can only really be healed when the self-healing process comes into play. All healing is ultimately self-healing, and no healer can do more than help to set this process in motion.

Underpinning the whole personal growth movement is a willingness to take responsibility for yourself, for your own health, emotions and way of being in the world. The various movements, organisations and self-help groups can help you to access and face up to the very core of your being, your own authentic self, and have the courage to take charge of your own life.

They cannot, of course, do your growing for you. All they can do, at most, is to point you in the right direction, to help you sort out the things which are important to you, and those which are simply wasting time or preventing genuine growth. There is no instant enlightenment, no easy, foolproof growth path, but the journey will be challenging, thought-provoking and exciting – and it will certainly enable you to put a new and more positive perspective on the things which have happened to you so far, and which might happen in the future.

Undertaking a personal growth journey will enable you to alter your own future for the better, and realise what genuine happiness and peace of mind is all about – a calm, thoughtful, introspective centre of your being which enables you to learn from the past, to set good actions in motion for the future, and to enjoy the present, whatever circumstances you may face. It enables you to detach and look at what is happening, to assess and take a clear look at all your relationships, and decide which ones are nurturing and supportive, and which are draining and energy-sapping.

As your journey progresses, you will find that you attract genuine friends, those who wish you well rather than trying to do you down. You will also gain immeasurably in confidence and self-respect.

Is it a journey that any of us can afford *not* to undertake?

Chapter 3

Personal Growth Organisations

Many of the organisations and movements described in this chapter – although by no means all – came into being in the 1960s, when the present-day personal growth movement first began to make rapid strides. At first, many people tended to regard these groups and organisations with extreme suspicion, and several were labelled dangerous cults.

But they have outlasted their critics, and have grown from strength to strength, because they are offering a way of life, an outlook or an experience that it is not possible to gain in ordinary, everyday life. They offer another view, another way of looking at things which, even if you decide you can't buy the whole package, will at least expand your consciousness, give you new input, and perhaps help you to get to know yourself that important bit better, and keep an open mind.

Some organisations exist to help you develop your personal talents and potential, whereas others, while facilitating personal growth, are geared more towards compassionate understanding of the world we live in. There are now very many environmental and ecological societies and organisations which have helped to raise consciousness of our relationship with the planet. Some of these have had outstanding success in alerting not just individuals, but also governments, to what we are doing to our planet, and how we can better harness the natural resources we have.

From the first, many of the organisations listed here attracted not just hippies and drop-outs, as some people imagine, those who couldn't seem to manage their lives in ordinary ways, but those who were above all seekers, people who felt that there might be a different and possibly better way of relating to one another, our families and the rest of humanity.

Most of the organisations listed here allow you to dip a toe into the field of personal growth, to see whether or not you feel inspired to take things further, without committing yourself to any lifelong changes or alterations.

(*Note*: There are so very many self-development and self-improvement courses and organisations these days that this section can only give space to some of them. I have tried to choose a representative selection, but this does not mean that those not mentioned are necessarily no good – only that they are similar to others described.)

The Aetherius Society

One of the earliest of the modern personal growth organisations, the Aetherius Society was founded by George King in 1955 to further interest in psychic matters and spiritual healing, at a time when they were widely scorned and derided.

The Society now runs a number of personal development, healing and psychic development courses. Its approach contains a mixture of Christianity, yoga, healing and spiritual techniques, with the aim of helping all interested people to find and fulfil themselves.

To some, the way the Society was founded may sound rather odd. George King, in common with Joan of Arc, Florence Nightingale and several others who have been similarly called, one day heard voices commanding him to become the Voice of Interplanetary Parliament. The voice came from a creature hailing from the planet Venus, called Aetherius.

The Society believes in life on other planets, and investigates UFOs. It takes reincarnation and astrology seriously. Its members are extremely active in the media, and at all New Age festivals. It attracts a lot of men, particularly those who are interested in inter-planetary matters, and who are trying to arrive at scientific proof that there is life on other planets.

International headquarters are at: 757 Fulham Road, London SW6 5UU. Tel: 071–736 4187.

Alternatives

This is a New Age organisation which holds meetings, workshops and seminars, mainly at the beautiful Wren church of St James in Piccadilly, itself a pioneer of open-mindedness among Christian churches. Most of the meetings, open to the general public, take place on Monday evenings from 7 to 9 p.m., and have a speaker who is an expert on some aspect of healing, New Age philosophy, poetry or ecology. This is followed by a question-and-answer session, and a chance to meet over supper.

The quality of the speakers is usually extremely high, and the organisation attracts eminent people from all over the world.

The evenings always start in the same way, with people being invited to shake hands and start up a brief conversation with the person sitting next to them. Candles are lit on themes chosen by the speaker of the evening, and there is usually five minutes of silent meditation.

The meetings are ideal for people who are curious about a particular subject, whether this is discussing addictions, the role of dolphins in healing, elves and fairies, sex in the forbidden zone, channelling information from discarnate entities, or the poetry of William Blake. Attendees can then decide whether they are interested enough to take the subject under discussion any further.

Further information from: Alternatives, St James's Church, 197 Piccadilly, London W1V 9LF. Tel: 071–287 6711.

Avatar

Avatar – the word is Hindu for a deity who voluntarily assumes physical form – is a course of study, first developed in 1979, to enable people to realise the fullest extent of their own creation, which is themselves. At the heart of the Avatar message is the idea that very many of us have denied our own full creative powers, or have misused them. The courses are designed to liberate the consciousness so that we can fully experience, understand and take charge of everything that happens to us, and direct our lives in ways that are more personally fulfilling than before.

The system teaches that we must believe in ourselves rather than in outside dogmas or precepts. Beliefs, says Harry Palmer, the American founder of the organisation, come in to substitute for personal responsibility. Because of what we have come to believe, both about ourselves and others, we put limits on what we imagine we can do.

Before anything else, we must discover the beliefs that work for us – then we can 'bring about our own reality', in a favourite New Age phrase. Basically, the courses, which last six days, and are held for groups of up to ten, are designed to free people from their previous hidebound belief systems which have, most probably without their realising it, hampered their personal growth and fulfilment.

Avatar, say its 'graduates', is not about religion, metaphysics or spiritualism. It does not concern God, channelled entities, angels or gurus. It is not a therapy, but students learn to 'discreate' the past by substituting genuine awareness of why things happen. It is designed to be a way of eliminating the root causes of our own limitations, and discovering what we are capable of after all.

Avatar is available world-wide and is now being used extensively by businesspeople who wish to increase their effectiveness in management.

Details from: Wendy Graham, 24 Ellerdale Road, Hampstead, London NW3 6BB. Tel: 071–794 9599.

Bath Associates

This is an organisation devoted to developing the spiritual side of business life, by encouraging those in large companies to become aware of aspects of themselves which they may have lost sight of in the scramble for business success.

The idea is that, by accessing their feminine, intuitive side, businesspeople will become more, not less, effective in their work. They will gain the confidence to take responsibility for themselves, to become compassionate towards others, to take risks and to reduce fear.

The seminars and workshops are concerned to enable delegates to become aware of certain abilities, and see them as important in the business world. They are the ability to be in touch with your emotions; to develop awareness of a wide range of feelings and to be able to discriminate accurately; to recognise your own emotional blindspots and dysfunctional emotional patterns; to be able to tolerate ambiguity and adverse feedback; to stay open to all kinds of feedback, whether positive or negative, and to be able to learn from it.

The Bath Programme, which is increasingly being viewed as a more modern alternative to the MBA, is an intensive course lasting eighteen months, and it is expensive – costing well over £3000. It is recognised by the University of Leicester as an advanced degree.

Details from: Bath Associates, 6 Vane Street, Bath, Avon BA2 4DZ. Tel: 0225 462835.

Brainwave

This is a practical organisation which publishes and markets New Age and spiritual information, books and courses. It also produces a package to help New Age businesses promote and market themselves, and can help if you are wondering whether or not your business or enterprise fits into New Age principles.

Brainwave publishes a number of holistic guides and catalogues, and can be useful for those who would like to know what exactly the differences are between a holistic, New Age approach and an 'old age' approach.

Information from: Brainwave, 33 Lorn Road, Stockwell, London SW9 0AB. Tel: 071–733 7883.

Breakthrough Centre

Many people find, when they attend one or two courses on personal growth, and are excited by the insights gained, that it can be difficult to carry out lessons learned in their careers. This Centre, established in 1988, is aimed at businesspeople who would like to know how to incorporate holistic and personal growth principles into every aspect of their lives, including their jobs.

This Centre is trying to build up an international business network on holistic principles, which it believes are far more effective and productive than the old ways of conducting business, which have had their day.

The Centre can provide help and support for those who are already employed, as well as people who wish to set up their own businesses conducted on personal growth and personal responsibility principles.

Details from: Breakthrough Centre, 7 Popular Mews, Uxbridge Road, London W12 7JS. Tel: 081–749 8525.

College of Psychic Studies

This College, situated in Kensington, West London, is open to anybody interested in examining the nature of psychic experience and coming to terms with their own psychic abilities. It runs a number of 'psychic unfolding' courses which are aimed at showing people how to make the best use of their psychic abilities, to become a medium or a healer, and how to harness these gifts for the good of all.

The College has always attracted the leading mediums and healers of its day, and now, after more than 60 years of existence, its courses are more popular than ever, as people are increasingly being able to admit and access their psychic abilities.

All you need to make a start is to be interested and open-minded about psychic matters. If you like, you can attend an open lecture – prices are very low – and then decide whether or not you wish to take it further. The College has an extensive bookshop, with leaflets, brochures and explanatory pamphlets.

The College believes we can all tap into our latent intuitive powers, and learn how to harness these to further loving relationships, gain greater self-knowledge, and increase our understanding of ourselves and others. It also believes there is no one single path to the truth, but that all the great spiritual traditions contain aspects of it. Since its inception, the College has encouraged people to get in touch safely with discarnate entities (spirits of people whose bodies have died, but who have not yet reincarnated).

People often join, or become interested in the College when a loved one has died, and they wish either to contact that person, or to discover why the loss has happened.

The College has always had strong bias towards women.

Details of courses in psychic unfoldment, spiritual healing, psychology, channelling and related matters from: The College of Psychic Studies, 16 Queensberry Place, London SW7 2EB. Tel: 071–589 3292/3.

Compassion in World Farming

This worldwide organisation is designed to raise public awareness of the cruelty and suffering involved in much factory farming. It tries to encourage farmers and others involved in the animal trade to use more humane methods of rearing and killing livestock.

For very many people, a love of animals is an initial way into personal growth and self-transformation. When people become aware that animals have feelings, and respond to kindness and cruelty, this can lead to greater compassion for humans as well.

CIWF, a charitable organisation, believes that when we allow cruelty to animals, we all become cruel and unfeeling, and shut off compassion and empathy. By increasing compassion in farming methods, we can increase love and a feeling of connectedness with all living creatures, which is one of the basic tenets of the whole personal growth movement.

This is a campaigning organisation, and donations are welcomed from animal lovers and those opposed to cruelty.

Details from: Compassion in World Farming, 20 Lavant Street, Petersfield GU32 3EW.

Encounter

Encounter groups first hit the headlines in the 1960s, as they were very different from any previous kind of group gathering. In the main, when we are in a group, we are encouraged to behave well, not to draw attention to ourselves, but to sit and listen politely, and to show respect for others in the group. In particular, if someone was doing something annoying, such as scratching his or her foot or tapping with a pencil, we might nervously request him or her to stop or, more usually, try to ignore it altogether.

The very opposite happened in Encounter groups. People were encouraged to get in touch with their feelings, to ask other members of the group why they felt constrained to act in a certain way, to go over and hug somebody, or perhaps kick his foot.

Encounter groups – which are basically a means for people to get to know themselves and others far better and more honestly – are still going today, but there is now a wider variety available. In some early groups, you were not allowed to leave the room even to go to the lavatory and, on residential courses, you hardly got any sleep.

There has been some loosening up since those days, but basically the idea of Encounter groups is to explore honest feelings, thoughts and expressions – even when these may be angry and hostile. The idea is that by working through anger and negativity, it can be dispelled and released. Encounter groups can last a day, a week or even a month.

Details about Encounter groups from: Open Centre, 188 Old Street, London EC1V 9BP. Tel: 081–549 9583.

(*Note*: The Open Centre, which is open seven days a week, is believed to be the UK's oldest-established growth centre and runs a wide variety of courses. Apart from Encounter groups, they include: individual and therapy sessions, psychodrama, transactional analysis and postural integration. (Transactional analysis works on the idea that we all play parts, such as those of the parent, child and adult, when interracting with other people. TA enables us to identify and define these roles and attitudes, in order to get to know ourselves better. Postural integration is a form of therapy which helps people to get back into bodily alignment, in the belief that we hold all kinds of repressions and neuroses in the way we walk, stand and sit.) The Centre is run collectively by its staff, and prices are kept as low as possible.)

Fellowship of the Inner Light

This is an organisation designed to help people expand their consciousness and maximise their potential. It was founded by Paul Solomon in Virginia Beach, USA, in 1972. The techniques he developed are designed to help people to achieve personal transformation.

The basic tenet of the Inner Light philosophy is that all genuine change must begin from within. In order to start taking responsibility, people must get into harmony with their inner selves, the source of their being.

The false self, says Paul Solomon, which most of us carry around all our lives, is formed by people reacting to us and telling us what we are, using words such as 'shy', 'talented', 'pretty' and so on. If we are told these things often enough by our parents and teachers, as most of us are, we grow up believing that they are true. Yet, they are usually somebody else's perception, and may have little bearing on the actual truth. We have to discover what we are like for ourselves.

Ninety per cent of people today, says Solomon, are living as victims, believing that they have no power whatever over their own lives, even their own thoughts. If we are unhappy, we believe that somebody or something has made us unhappy; if we are unsuccessful, it's because 'luck' has not gone our way.

Yet all of us can call on our 'higher gifts' and develop these, to become the kind of people we would most like to be. The Fellowship says it is one step beyond Encounter groups and awareness training in that it enables people to bring about change from within rather than by behavioural modification methods, which Solomon sees as only temporary, and not genuinely empowering.

The inner reality, says Solomon, creates the outer reality. Inner Light courses, which are held at the Society's headquarters, are designed to enable people to trust their intuition, imagination and every aspect of their consciousness, to live life to the full, and to learn to love oneself and others properly, and to spread happiness and cheerfulness to everyone we come across in our daily lives.

That, says Paul Solomon, is true success, rather than the flashier achievements of being a famous politician, architect, tycoon or whatever.

Ultimately, says Paul Solomon, we shall be judged by the amount of life and love we are able to create in our small corners of the world. The Fellowship does not adhere to any particular dogma, but has a definite spiritual side.

The Fellowship runs courses, seminars, weekend workshops, retreats and lectures on such subjects as unconditional love, inner guidance, spiritual discernment, journeys to sacred sites, healing, Bible studies.

Details from: Fil-UK, PO Box 23, Camberley, Surrey GU17 7FT. Tel: 0344 761445.

Festival of Mind, Body and Spirit

This Festival, which has been going since 1977, has provided an intro-duction to New Age and alternative philosophies for many British people. Its offshoots have spread to America, Australia and several European countries.

It was the brainchild of Graham Wilson, who still runs and oversees the organisation. He was a former marketing consultant, who had a deep and abiding interest in New Age and personal growth ideas when they were considered somewhat strange and cranky. The Festival was a resounding success from the start, and eventually Graham dropped all his other work to concentrate on planning it, and related events, full time. By the early 1980s, he was running similar Festivals in New York, Los Angeles, San Francisco and Australia.

The format of the Festivals has changed a great deal from the early days, to reflect the growing interest in personal development and self-transformation. At first, it was the stands and stalls which were most popular, as to many people they opened up a completely new world, that of crystal and spiritual healing, tarot cards, aura healing and so on.

Now, ever more people are becoming willing to dip more than a toe into the whole area, and are signing up for the workshops, seminars and lectures. Graham Wilson also runs a natural health clinic at his headquar-ters in Kensington, London, and this has become extremely popular as well. He says:

'In the 1960s there was the first flowering of these ideas. Once people's basic needs have been met, they can then go on to explore the more spiritual, emotional and mental aspects of themselves. There is a great and growing dissatisfaction with present day society, a feeling that there must be more to life than this.

'Something very important happened in the 1960s, when people first began to tune in, turn on and drop out. Most people had never had the confidence to do anything like this before, but simply followed in the footsteps of their parents and grandparents.

'But now the movement has grown up, and people are managing to combine their work, family and everyday life with personal growth. The ideas that seemed so strange in the 1960s, those of working in harmony with your environment, of being co-operative rather than intensely compe-titive, are now being integrated into offices and workplaces. It has become

a whole way of life for ever more people, and is still growing.
    'In order for the new to emerge, the old had to collapse – and we are now seeing this happen.'

As well as the yearly Festival, Graham Wilson's organisation, New Life Designs, runs healing arts exhibitions, and a wide range of seminars, workshops and residential retreats.

Details and programmes from: The Secretary, Arnica House, 170 Campden Hill Road, London W8 7AS. Tel: 071–938 3788.

Findhorn

Findhorn is a thriving alternative community in an inhospitable corner of North-east Scotland. It attracts visitors from all over the world and many people have found it an inspiration indeed, as it is a highly successful community of several hundred people, who live completely 'alternatively' and yet highly successfully, proving that there is a different, yet effective, way of doing things.

The Community, which has a flourishing business and enterprise section, is founded on principles of love and respect for all living things. It is completely democratic, and no decisions are made until everybody in the 'inner circle' is unanimous. Every member of the community receives the same minimal amount of money each month, and everyone helps with chores, bookkeeping, running courses and so on. The Community, founded in the 1960s, has always had a name for creative endeavours, and its pottery and art studios produce high-quality work which is sold all over the world.

The way the Community started is strange enough. Its founders, Eileen and Peter Caddy and Dorothy McLean, were running an hotel when suddenly they were all given the sack – and four hours to leave the premises. All they had was a caravan and a car. They set off with the Caddys' three children – Eileen already had five children from a previous marriage whom she had not seen for several years – to Findhorn Caravan Park, where they lived on national assistance, the forerunner of income support.

Peter could not find a job, and none of the three knew what would happen next. But one day Eileen heard a voice saying: 'Know that I am

God.' This voice told her to plant a wonderful garden round their caravan. As nothing whatever grew at Findhorn, which was basically a windswept, sandy beach, it seemed a peciliar enough command. But Peter Caddy, who had had a lifelong interest in spiritual and psychic matters, obeyed the instructions and, with his national assistance money, bought seeds and fertiliser.

Eventually, a garden grew that became, literally, one of the wonders of the world. Botanists and horticulturalists came and inspected it, and said it was impossible: nothing whatever could grow in the poor, sandy soil. And yet it did.

From those tiny beginnings grew a community which runs residential courses in all aspects of personal growth, in alternative business and ecology methods, in fulfilling personal potential and living in harmony with one's fellow humans and non-humans, and developing spiritual awareness.

The Community is founded basically on Christian lines, but it is not the kind of Christianity which would be readily recognised by the Church of England, for instance.

I went to Findhorn a few years ago in an attitude of great scepticism and cynicism, and came back wiser and with an enormously increased self-knowledge, even after a week. The courses are highly structured, and follow a set path, in that you have to do introductory courses before you can move on to those concentrating more intensively on personal transformation. Course participants are encouraged to see each other as brothers and sisters, to hug, to be open and honest about feelings, to say 'I' instead of 'one' or 'you' when referring to your self or offering an opinion, and to be confident about connecting with nature and the nature spirits.

Participants have to join in the chores – cleaning, cooking, washing up – as no outside staff are employed. The Community now owns the hotel, known as Cluny College, from which the founders were once sacked, the whole caravan park, and many other properties in the area around Forres – a place mentioned in *Macbeth*.

Findhorn is likely to appeal to somebody interested in the concept of personal growth and who is open-minded enough to give the concept of living in a truly sharing community a try. Most people have to share bedrooms, and this is one of the aspects of personal growth – you have to do your level best to get on with everybody.

Courses are all residential, and can last a week, several weeks, several months, or even years.

Details from: Findhorn Foundation, The Park, Forres IV36 0TZ.
Tel: 0309 73655.

The Foundation for Global Unity

This is a group of people who have come together to try and improve the
quality of life for themselves and others in the world today. The Foundation is a fairly loose structure consisting of healers, astrologers, spirit-
ualists and clairvoyants who teach reincarnation and karmic law. The
Foundation does not hold courses, but sees interested people individually, or in groups. They will provide astrology charts, they teach I
ching, the ancient Chinese method of helping people to come to terms
with their personal problems, and they also have a team of 'time travellers'
who help to search for missing people and stolen or lost goods.

This Foundation tries to put people in touch with the best person to
help them with a particular problem. Their speciality is reincarnation
readings from the Akashic records – a supposed 'log book' of all the
actions and deeds or misdeeds of everybody who has ever lived or will live
on the planet.

Information from: The Foundation for Global Unity, Abbey Lodge
Guest House, 8 New Dover Road, Canterbury, Kent CT1 3AP. Tel:
0227 462878.

Gaia

This is a theory about how our planet works which was postulated by
Professor James Lovelock in 1969. Strictly speaking, there should be
nothing left of the planet by now as the laws of thermodynamics ought to
mean that it would have disintegrated into an inert, lifeless mass. Yet, it
hasn't. Somehow, it keeps renewing itself and life goes on.

Professor Lovelock's theory is that planet Earth comprises a
complete, self-supporting and self-renewing system which will always
operate, somehow. He studied the biosphere (the plants and creatures
on earth), the lithosphere (the solid portion) and the atmosphere, and
came to the conclusion that it all combined to create an integrated

system. It was, in fact, a living entity with everything intertwined and interdependent.

Lovelock called his theory the Gaia Hypothesis, after the Greek Goddess of the earth. The concept of Gaia is intimately linked to that of personal growth, as it means we are all part of the same system, individual and yet related to every organic and even inorganic entity on earth. We are all part of it, not separate from it.

Information from: Alternatives, St James Church, 197 Piccadilly, London W1V 9LF. Tel: 071–287 6711.

The Hen House (women only)

Here, even the cats are female! The Hen House was set up by Rachel Lever, a former artist and political activist, who felt the time had come to set up a hotel and conference centre where women could come together, find themselves and establish sisterly links with each other. It is a place where consciousness can be raised and where women can feel at peace in their surroundings, unhampered by the attentions of the opposite sex.

There are courses on the creative arts, recovery from addiction or 'loving too much', growing old disgracefully, aromatherapy, exercise and sport, yoga and relaxation. The idea is to facilitate personal growth through women all meeting together and sharing their experiences, and growing together rather than being isolated, as women still often are, from each other.

The courses are all residential, and meals are provided. The idea, said Rachel Lever, was that women could come together, explore their lives and where they were at, expand their personal potential, listen to lectures, attend workshops and retreats, and get to know what they really wanted out of life. There are numerous courses on exploring all aspects of our relationships, with our parents, partners, children and workmates – and coming to terms with these.

The Hen House may appeal to those women who do not perhaps feel ready to plunge themselves into something completely unknown and different, such as Findhorn, but who would welcome the opportunity to get away from their everyday cares and worries in a peaceful, tranquil setting, to explore aspects of their lives which, until now, have not been fully thought through.

Situated on the North Lincolnshire coast, the Hen House attracts single, married and partnered women from all over the country, from a wide range of backgrounds, and provides a genuine opportunity to be sisterly. The hotel accommodation is comfortable and roomy, and expansion is going on all the time.

Details and brochures from: The Hen House, Hawerby Hall, nr Thoresby, Lincs DN36 5QL. Tel: 0472 840278.

Insight

Insight personal development seminars, like very many other personal growth organisations, started in America. There are now branches of Insight throughout most of Europe, and in Australia and South America. They are run as basically six-day courses, where participants can find out how to lead much more satisfying lives by developing their self-confidence, belief in themselves and their abilities, to have better relationships with everybody they meet.

The starting point for the seminars is that many, possibly most of us, are holding ourselves back and preventing ourselves from living fulfilling lives. The seminars consist of one-to-one and group work, creative visualisation and guided imagery. (Visualisation is the ability to see in imagination how things should be, or how you would like them to be. For instance, if you want to be well, you imagine yourself having a fit and healthy body, and keep that image constantly in front of you. You do not allow thought of a sick, diseased body to take over your mind. If you want to be rich, you imagine yourself as already a rich person, rather than the poor one you may be at the moment.)

There is no set charge, but in 1993 a figure of £350 is recommended for the six-day seminars in their explanatory brochures. If you don't like the course, or feel you have not benefited at all, you are entitled to your money back.

Information about Insight from: 37 Spring Street, London W2 1JA. Tel: 071–706 2021. Introductory lectures are held free of charge in London hotels in the West End.

International Association for Near-Death Studies and the Natural Death Centre

How can death contribute to personal growth – and living in the here and now? Over the past few years, great attention has been paid by those interested in personal growth to death, near-death and to our own attitudes towards death, which can be so restricting that they prevent us from living fully. So many of us are afraid of death, and this fear stops us from enjoying the present as much as we could.

The International Association (IANDS) began when it was increasingly being realised that many patients on life-support machines were experiencing a near-death experience, where they had a sense of euphoria and of floating out of their bodies, through a tunnel and into light. In the old days, of course, they would have died, but since life-support machines began to be used, many came through, and lived to tell the tale.

IANDS was set up by doctors, scientists and psychiatrists to further research into the subject, and try to assess its significance to those undergoing it. Most, if not all people, who have undergone a near-death experience, find that it appears to illuminate their whole lives, give them new insights, allows them to have more empathy and compassion, and allows them to see clearly what was dark, hidden or obscure before. The studies and case-histories on this are now numerous.

According to Margot Grey, author of *Return from Death*, an account of both her own near-death experience and a review of the literature and research on the subject, it is common for fundamental life changes to take place after such an experience. For one thing, the memory of the experience stays clear and undimmed by the passing years. There is also, commonly, a great sense of renewal and purpose in life. Enhanced self-esteem and self-confidence are also common after such an event, although it may seem a rather drastic way of self-improvement.

After a near-death experience, people often find that their relationships with others are improved, and they become more compassionate and tolerant. There is a definite sense of being reborn, of being given another chance, and a renewed determination to live life to the full. Material considerations are no longer quite so important, and love and service to humanity take their place. There is a heightened sense of love and rapport with others, a feeling that the cosmos has an established

65

order, rather than being random and chaotic, and that everything has a purpose. In fact, all the aspects of personal growth are usually contained in this one vivid experience.

Also, very often, inherent gifts and talents that have not been previously fully used come to the fore. For many people, the near-death experience brings about an awareness that these gifts have been given to us for the service of others, and yet there is no ego involved, or wish for personal fame or fortune. The fear of death is greatly diminished, and along with this vanishes any fear of illness or of losing one's faculties.

Information about the near-death experience and IANDS from: IANDS UK, PO Box 193, London SW1K 9JZ.

The Natural Death Centre was formed to research alternatives to euthanasia, by allowing people to choose to pass away when they felt that they did not want to go on living any longer. The Centre has now enlarged its activities to provide courses and seminars that enable people to come to terms with death, both their own and of other people, and break the current taboos surrounding physical death.

The Centre was founded by psychologists, and also concentrates on researching and collecting accounts of near-death and dignified death, and helping people to draw up 'living wills' which will allow relatives and doctors to suspend treatment if they are suffering from a terminal or painful condition, or have lost the will to carry on living.

The Natural Death Centre explores all dignified ways of dying, alternative funeral services, reusable coffins, cheap funerals, memorial groves, making your own coffins – and all the aspects of death previously considered morbid and, therefore, little talked about or faced.

Information and fact sheets: The Natural Death Centre, 20 Heber Road, London NW2 6AA. Tel: 081–208 2853. Fax: 081–452 6434.

Isis

Isis run workshops for women with the purpose of unlocking previously hidden creative and life-affirming powers. There are also workshops on creative journal-keeping. Keeping a diary can be seen as a way of assisting personal growth, so long as you don't use it just to record miserable events. But, with a new consciousness, keeping a diary can be seen as a way to chart progress, and to keep a record of what we are feeling now. It allows us to compare our feelings and emotions at some distance from an important event, with what they were like at the time.

Anybody who has ever kept a diary, who wonders however people keep up the effort, or who has enjoyed dipping into teenage revelations, may be interested in these workshops. The concept behind the creative journal, according to workshop founder Simona Parker, is an amalgam of the theories of Jung, Assagioli and Abraham Maslow.

Details from: Simona Parker. Tel: 081–995 5320.

Landmark Education

An offshoot of EST, the Encounter-type seminars established by Warner Erhard in California which has now changed its name to Forum.

Landmark is a one-day self-improvement course aimed at businesspeople and run on Encounter-type lines. People pour out their career troubles and difficulties, and often break down in tears. Participants are allowed to leave the room only once every three hours, and the course lasts from 8.45 a.m. until 11 p.m.

As with other aspects of est, Landmark has been on the receiving end of much adverse publicity, but anyway it goes on, and people find benefit from being given permission to talk about what is deeply bothering them. Est has been called a dangerous cult, but there is little evidence of any harm being done by the methods used.

In 1993 the course costs £150 for the day.

Information from: Landmark Trust, 21 Deans Yard, London SW1P 3PA. Tel: 071–222 6581.

Loving Relationships Training

The LRT was devised by American psychologist Sondra Ray, a pupil of Leonard Orr, one of the instigators of rebirthing (see *Healing* section).

The purpose of this training is to help people develop better relationships in their personal and professional lives.

But before we can have good relationships with others, we must love ourselves and see ourselves as inherently lovable and worthy of respect. Unless we can appreciate this, we will tend to fall into patterns of self-sacrifice and self-sabotage, thus diminishing ourselves. Then, we never gain the love we are so desperately seeking.

The LRT, which runs quite expensive weekend courses (running into several hundred pounds), shows participants how to release and reverse old patterns of behaviour which may go right back to birth. The idea is that you go back to the source of your problems, locate them and then release them so that they no longer exert their baleful influence on your current relationships.

The idea behind LRT weekends is that you are given a 'lasting experience of your inherent attractiveness, worth and potential'. Most people I know who have been on an LRT weekend have said that it transformed their lives greatly for the better, and was well worth the expense.

Information from: LRT, Flat D, 9 Claverton Street, London SW1V 3AY. Tel: 071–834 6641. Cost of a weekend in 1993: approximately £450.

Lucis Trust

This was established to further the work and writings of Alice Bailey, who during her lifetime wrote a total of twenty-four books on esoteric philosophy. It is dedicated to creating a 'new world order' of brotherhood, co-operation and right relationships. The Trust runs correspondence courses, has audio and video-recordings, and branches in most countries in the world.

The basic idea of the Trust is to enable people to become aware of the spiritual side of their natures, and see these as more important than bodily or material aspects. The key word of the Trust is 'discipleship', which means the ability to listen to what your soul is saying, and impose its will on the 'lower nature', rather than the other way round.

The Trust and its various offshoots, such as the Arcane School, are working to try and heal the rifts between people, and to enable us to see that we are all brothers and sisters, all connected, all sharing in the same basic humanity. Points of similarity, rather than differences, are emphasised. The Trust believes, as with most other personal growth organisations, that humanity is evolving to a plan, and that nothing is haphazard or chaotic, even if it often seems so.

Meetings are held fortnightly in the Charing Cross Hotel, there is a free lending library at the Trust's HQ, and regular lectures are held on meditation, healing, ecology, metaphysics. The Trust now has consultative status with the United Nations.

Information about correspondence courses from: Lucis Trust, Suite 54, 3 Whitehall Court, London SW1 2EF. Tel: 071–839 4512.

Outward Bound

The very term 'Outward Bound' conjures up images of abseiling down rocks, spending nights on cold mountainsides without watch or compass, of having cold showers, communal dorms and Spartan meals. It must be said that there is a great deal of truth in this image, even though Outward Bound has become a lot more comfortable since its early days.

The movement was founded by Kurt Hahn who also started Gordonstoun School on similar principles. His philosophy was that the best way of conquering deep-seated fears and phobias was to face up to tough physical challenges.

Today, there are very many Outward Bound courses in many countries in the world, where the emphasis is on personal growth and development. There are now special courses, each lasting about a week, for women, for business executives, for disabled and handicapped people, for those at the start of their careers, and for all those who wish to be more effective in their everyday lives.

Kurt Hahn's philosophy can be summed up in his most famous quote: 'We are all better than we know. If only we can be brought to realise this, we may never be prepared to settle for anything less.'

The idea behind Outward Bound is that through facing tough physical challenges, where the dangers are always more apparent than real, you can come to know yourself, realise that you may have been limiting yourself far more than you need, and have most probably been handicapping yourself without fully realising it.

You do not have to be super-fit to attend an Outward Bound course, nor do you have to be able to swim and climb, or have a background of rugged outdoor activity. In fact, most people attending the courses are individuals leading sedentary, indoor lives, and who are interested in trying something different, something they have never attempted before.

The courses are suitable for people of all ages and fitness levels, so long as you do not have a serious chronic condition. You can take things at your own pace and, on all the courses, there is mutual friendship and support. Fears and self-doubts vanish as, one by one, the physical challenges are faced and overcome.

There are five centres in the UK, all set in beautiful surroundings, and the Trust also runs City Challenge courses, where able-bodied people have placements with the disabled and handicapped. The Trust is a registered charity, and prices are kept low.

Information from: Outward Bound, Chestnut Field, Regent Place, Rugby CV21 2PJ. Tel: 0788 560423.

Schumacher College

The College, which opened in 1991 in the buildings of the former Dartington School, Devon, is dedicated to promoting the work and ideals of E. F. Schumacher, author of *Small is Beautiful: Economics as Though People Mattered*. The main function of the College, which runs a number of residential courses, is to look at valid alternatives to socialism, capitalism and all the other 'isms' which dominate contemporary politics.

E. F. Schumacher believed that much of the scientific and rational world view that governs contemporary life is actually impoverishing and dehumanising, for the individual, for countries and for the world. Capitalism, for instance, makes a very few people rich and most people poor. The conventional nuclear family isolates women and promotes men as the breadwinners at the expense of women, so that roles become polarised and what men do seems more important than what women do.

At the same time, capitalism fosters greed, destruction of the planet and ruins traditional cultures, which in many cases had been coping perfectly well for centuries, until 'modernisation' appeared, with its seductive promises of cars, washing machines, education, material prosperity for all – none of which has happened for most developing countries.

The trouble with 'Westernisation' is that it looks very attractive from the outside – people appear rich and prosperous, and don't seem to have to work all that hard for a living. When people from traditional societies see rich tourists with their cameras and shellsuits, they want these for themselves. They become dissatisfied with their own culture, and the result is monoculture – the same bland international hotels, buildings, roads, clothes, soft drinks – all over the world.

The idea of most Western governments is that in order to be successful, economies must 'grow'. Usually, this is interpreted as producing more material goods. The problem is, the growth is unlikely to be sustainable – most of the much-coveted material goods are constructed out of materials which are eventually going to be used up, as they are not renewable. Oil, steel, coal and so on are finite entities, even if the initial supply is large.

Schumacher College runs courses for those who wish to consider workable alternatives, and to see how these can be achieved. Its courses are aimed at people who are interested in global matters as well as their own personal growth, as these are seen to go together.

Thinking about ways of sustainable growth, modest initiatives which are applicable to the particular country and the people, rather than trying to force blanket Westernisation on to countries which simply can't adopt it, also means that people start thinking about themselves, how they relate to the world, whether they are contributing to, or spoiling the earth. So, personal consciousness is raised at the same time as global issues are discussed.

The courses have been designed to be quite different from those at a standard college or university, and comprise four main elements: *scholarship*, a detailed study of the central theme under scrutiny; *community*, where participants and lecturers work together and interconnect with each other; *meditation*, a quiet time set aside to ponder on the matters discussed during the daytime; and *work*, similar to that at Findhorn, where staff and participants cook, clean and tend the garden.

The courses are emotionally as well as intellectually demanding, as participants have to start examining their often long-held attitudes and beliefs.

The College emphatically points out that it is not primarily a therapeutic or personal growth centre, but acknowledges that personal growth almost always takes place. Satish Kumar, the College's director, also edits the New Age magazine *Resurgence*, whose circulation has grown from 500 to almost 10,000 since he took over in the mid-1970s.

71

Information from: Schumacher College, The Old Postern, Dartington, Totnes, Devon TQ9 6EA. Tel: 0803 865934. Fax: 0803 866899.

Skyros Centre

This is a well-established personal growth and holiday centre set in the Greek island of Skyros. There is an intensive programme of yoga and meditation available, and also personal development courses on Gestalt, bioenergeics, psychodrama (see *Healing Treatments* section for details about these). Courses cost from just over £400 to £500, excluding flights.

Information from: Skyros Centre, Prince of Wales Road, London NW5 2NE. Tel: 071–267 4424/431 0867.

The Silva Method

Silva was developed by Latin-American engineer José Silva and is a way of accessing the intuitive aspects of our brain, so that we can understand and follow this authentic inner voice.

It is a kind of creative, directed daydreaming, and has become popular all over the world. For many people, it is a step on the way for those who have started to become interested in their own personal growth and in maximising their potential.

The whole point of the Silva Method is to awaken the unused talents of the mind. Basically, the course takes place over a weekend, consists of 30 hours of lecturing and 10 hours of mental exercises to teach people how to relax the mind and body, and concentrates on helping people to function more effectively.

The Method can be used to control pain, speed up healing, abandon unwanted habits and develop the sixth sense. The result of all this is (or should be) a sense of inner peace, a greater optimism and release of pent-up creativity.

The opportunity to do all this happens, according to the Method, when we learn to go into a deep meditative level – quite different from being asleep as this form of meditation takes concentration – and train our minds to go into the alpha mode, which is the brainwave where creativity happens.

José Silva was born in 1914, in Laredo, Texas, and his father died when he was four. He became the family breadwinner at an early age, and earned a living repairing radios. Soon, his repair business became one of the largest in the area. He studied to become an instructor in the Signal Corps during the Second World War, and afterwards built up his repair business again. He took a teaching job at Laredo Junior College and there he became interested in hypnotism.

During his investigations into hypnosis, he wondered whether IQ could be increased through conscious training. He already knew from his studies that the mind generates electricity, and believed that the brain's alpha rhythms offered less resistance than other rhythms. Our basic waking rhythm is the beta frequency, which is the fastest and is associated with left-brain, conscious thinking. Alpha comes next and, when we are asleep, the waves slow down to delta and theta. The letters of the Greek alphabet by which the brain waves are known refers to the order in which they were discovered.

José Silva learned that while hypnotism permits receptivity to some extent, the crucial problem with altered consciousness is how to keep the brain alert and functioning, rather than just responding and reacting. He eventually abandoned hypnosis, which is basically a giving-over of the conscious mind to unconscious processes, and began experimenting with conscious mental training.

He was able to develop a method whereby the mind can be trained to go into alpha at will, and then decided to teach this to other people. He started off with his own children – he has ten altogether, several of whom are now active in Silva Method work – and gradually expanded it to other people's children and then adults.

From this, he developed his method of dynamic, or active, meditation, which is now used all over the world. Dynamic meditation, Silva came to realise, has its own laws. In order for an event to come about, three elements must be present: you must *believe* in it; you must *desire* it; and you must *expect* it. The method will work only with good or positive plans, and will not be able to bring evil events into being. Silva also emphasizes that we should use the Method only for the important things in life, so as not to dilute the source.

The Silva Method can be used for speed learning, for creative sleep – using dreams to solve specific problems – and also makes use of Couéism (a system of optimistic auto-suggestion), where you repeat to yourself: every day in every way I am getting better and better.

The Silva Method, which has been going since 1966, has been investigated in a number of clinical trials and found to be extremely effective.

The courses are quite expensive (over £300 for a weekend in 1993), but there is a money-back guarantee if you are not satisfied. Courses are held in London, Glasgow and Manchester at selected hotels (non-residential), and there are free introductory lectures held at a number of venues throughout the year. The basic lecture course lasts for four days, from 9.30 a.m. to 7 p.m. There are also advanced courses on money philosophy, having charisma and on how to be even more effective.

The organisation also publishes a newsletter and, having attended a basic seminar, you can always attend others anywhere in the world for no extra charge.

Details from: The Silva Method, 216 Heaton Moor Road, Stockport, Cheshire SK4 4DU. Tel: 061–431 0001. Fax: 061 443 2380.

Society for Psychical Research

This is not strictly a personal growth organisation as it does not run self-development or self-transformation courses, or indeed, courses of any kind, although it does hold lectures and seminars at its headquarters. There is also an extensive psychic library which can be consulted by members. Since its inception in 1882, the Society has always attracted leading names in scientific and research fields.

Information from: The Society for Psychical Research, 1 Adam and Eve Mews, London W8 6UG. Tel: 071–937 8984.

Turning Points

This organisation was set up in 1982 by Sabine Kurjo McNeill with the purpose of holding lectures, workshops and conferences on the theme of transforming consciousness. Speakers come from many parts of the world to talk about new directions in medicine and healing, taking responsibility, changing ourselves and looking at ways to remain healthy. There is an emphasis on medical matters, and many speakers at the conference are doctors and scientists who take a holistic and spiritual approach to health.

For information on forthcoming conferences and lectures, contact: Turning Points, 21a Goldhurst Terrace, London NW6 3HB. Tel: 071–625 8804.

Universitas Associates

This is a small group of doctors, psychologists, astrologers and healers who concentrate on helping people with their personal growth through the use of ESP (extra-sensory perception) and mediumistic powers. Although the connection between character and astrological position has not yet been proved – in fact, most studies which have tried to prove a connection have not been successful – many people feel that the method is accurate or, at least, has value.

Perhaps the best way to regard astrology is as a tool, a way in, in much the same way as crystals or tarot cards may be. At the very least, an astrological and psychological reading is interesting – it can be regarded as another way of counselling which helps you to find out what you want.

For further information: Tel: 081–643 4898. Universitas Associates only sees people on a one-to-one basis.

Westminster Pastoral Foundation

This organisation was instrumental in establishing the whole counselling business in the UK. Counselling is basically a development of psycho-therapy, but concentrates on specific issues in a person's life, rather than generalised dissatisfaction or unhappiness. Most often, people come to counselling when they are going through a profound crisis in their lives, and when they want to talk to somebody who is trained to listen.

Effective counselling can lead to profound growth and change, but it is important to select people who are properly trained counsellors, as it may be possible to do more harm than good when dealing with deep emotions.

Counselling may be held in one-to-one, group or family sessions, and anybody in trouble can always find a sympathetic listener at the WPF.

The WPF runs a large number of courses, for those wishing to become professional counsellors, those who want to understand the basics of counselling and people who would like to become more effective listeners. There is also a wide variety of help groups for those with particular needs, such as people who feel lonely, those who have suffered bereavement, the loss of a job or a traumatic end to a relationship.

Information about courses, seminars, training programmes from: Westminster Pastoral Foundation, 23 Kensington Square, London W8 5HN. Tel: 071–937 6956.

(*Note*: This list of personal growth organisations cannot hope to be exhaustive, but gives an idea of the range of courses, seminars and lectures currently available. For guidance on more specific matters concerning personal growth, such as spiritual development, healing or self-help, read the relevant sections of this book.)

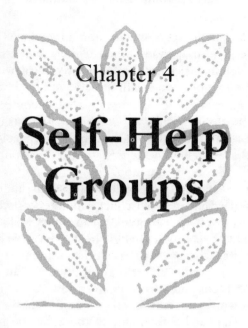

Chapter 4

Self-Help Groups

Self-help groups are, to my mind, among the most important strands of the personal growth movement. For, although at times we may need the help of a professional therapist or an established organisation, there are also occasions when nobody can help us but ourselves.

Self-help groups are not exactly new: the first one, for alcoholics, began life in America as long ago as the 1930s. The idea, completely revolutionary then, was that the best person to help an alcoholic was another alcoholic. But the idea was slow to take off until the early 1980s, when self-help groups for people in all kinds of trouble and difficulty gradually became a large, world-wide force.

Nowadays, self-help groups are often seen as a good starting-point for those whose lives have become difficult, or who feel that there is nobody else who understands them. For, whereas professional therapists, psychologists and psychiatrists have probably not experienced the particular problem for themselves, the point about self-help groups is that everybody attending is, or has been, in exactly the same boat.

In a self-help group, you can be sure that everybody present will not only be interested in what you have to say, they will also closely identify with it – because they have been there themselves. Also, there will be no judgement, no feeling among the group that you could have pulled yourself together and done things differently. You will feel immediately that you are among friends, among like-minded people.

77

In a self-help group, you will all be working together. Of course, some people will be further along the road to recovery than others, but all will understand the deep-seated and long-standing problems which are not easily extricated by a mere act of will.

For, whereas a non-alcoholic doctor may soon become sick and tired of a patient who persistently drinks too much when he has been repeatedly advised to cut down his intake, another alcoholic will precisely understand the nature of the addiction, which is, that it is stronger than you – otherwise it wouldn't be an addiction.

Many people are now asking serious questions about the value of psychotherapy and psychoanalysis: in fact, a number of psychotherapists in America have now given up their work because they feel it does not get to the heart of people's problems. The self-help movement has, by contrast, been one of the great therapy success stories of the past few decades.

Through an appropriate self-help group, people can identify exactly what is troubling them and why, and work towards some kind of permanent recovery with support from other members of the group. But just as there is no instant enlightenment, so there can be no guarantee of instant recovery from compulsive behaviour. There will often be a great deal of denial, resistance and dishonesty from new participants. All the other people in the group will understand this – because they have behaved in exactly the same way.

Self-help groups provide safe places where you can shed your secrets, admit things to yourself and to others in the group that you have possibly never dared to face up to before. Self-help groups are not always the answer to life's problems, but they have not yet been bettered for those suffering from some kind of compulsive, repetitive behaviour which is gradually making their lives hell.

As the majority of self-help groups exist to try and assist people to overcome addictions of one sort or another, I will deal with these first, and then move on to self-help groups for people suffering from serious or chronic illness. There are now many, many groups for parents with children who have serious problems – hyperactivity, Down's syndrome, cystic fibrosis, for instance. For many such parents, joining a self-help organisation lets them know they are not alone, and that they do not have to cope alone.

Lastly, I will describe what is happening with women's and men's consciousness-raising groups of various kinds in the 1990s. Although much work has been done, consciousness is not so universally raised that we can yet afford to sit on our laurels.

The point about self-help groups is that they enable people who are working to a similar goal, or who have similar problems, to meet and discuss ways of overcoming these. They are ways of becoming your own expert – and those who belong to such groups discover after a time that the knowledge, power and insights they have gained give them the power and confidence to address their problem head on.

Addictions

As it is increasingly being understood that addictions of one kind or another – to drink, drugs, gambling, sex, codependency (where you try to get your needs met by pleasing and rescuing other people), overspending, overeating or other forms of self-sabotage – are often at the very heart of people's difficulties, I shall start off by describing the work of the various 'anonymous' organisations and their offshoots. These organisations work to try and help people separate themselves from their addictions, and help them towards lifelong sobriety and manageability.

It seems overwhelmingly self-evident to me that addictions are the curse of our age, and the main reason why so very many of us cannot seem to function properly, form healthy relationships or get to love and know ourselves. But this explanation is certainly not accepted by mainstream psychiatry. Also, some branches of feminism reject the addictions idea, believing (wrongly, in my view) that to label women addictive, or dysfunctional, is to see them as victims, powerless in their own lives.

But the point about addictions is that eventually they do make people powerless – and completely unable even to start to see themselves, other people and even society, in any objective way.

The whole subject of addictions has been the focus of intense research in America since the early 1980s, and has spawned a huge number of books and self-help organisations aiming at helping people to recognise and then free themselves from what eventually becomes an all-pervading problem, affecting every corner of sufferers' lives – and the lives of their families. It has been estimated that one addict affects, on average, eight other people's lives.

The whole field of addictions has been such a growth industry, and so many best-selling books have been written on the subject (mainly hailing from America, the addiction republic of the world), that already there has been a backlash, with people complaining that by identifying and naming addictions, we are creating problems where there were none before.

I do not go along with this view. I believe that a growing knowledge of addictions has been one of the major breakthroughs in understanding the human condition over the past few years. I believe that the language of addictive behaviour, with words such as denial, codependency, shame and guilt, can enable us to appreciate and understand much that may have seemed inexplicable before.

An understanding of the addictive nature of our problems is not exactly new. In fact, it started way back in the 1930s with the formation of Alcoholics Anonymous, and the development of the 12-Step programme, which is still the only effective recovery programme in existence.

So, what are addictions, and why do they create so much damage? Why are they so very powerful that they gain an enormous hold on our lives and behaviour, gradually destroying everything?

We are addicted when we can't say no. The word 'addiction' comes from the Latin for 'to speak' and means, literally, that you can't speak, you have no power over the substance or activity. You are held in its grip.

To be addicted means to be controlled by a substance, a person or an emotion. When we are addicted, we become robotic, like all other addicts, eventually only able to stumble our way from one fix to the next. We lose our power of choice. At the same time, we blame everybody else for how we are. 'It was a woman who drove me to drink,' said W. C. Fields, and added: 'and I never had the grace to thank her.' All addicts tend to blame other people for their addiction – it's one of the symptoms of the disease.

All kinds of behaviour and substances – anything that has the power to alter our thinking, emotions or behaviour – have addiction potential. Anything which produces a high degree of excitement, which can calm us down, result in alteration of consciousness, can cause addictive behaviour. Some people may be addicted to food, others to alcohol and others to apparently exciting or needy people – the codependents.

We can become addicted to sex, to working hard, to shopping or to gambling. It seems as if, on the whole, it is the more highly sensitive, or perhaps more troubled, people who are most likely to succumb to addictions. Addicts are often found in the artistic fields of writing, painting and music. Highly creative people appear to be more at risk than those who are 'earthed' and content.

What happens with addiction is that it results in progressive alienation from the self. In fact, the addiction itself starts from a base of low self-esteem and self-dislike. People start to become addicts when they don't like themselves as they are when sober. They want to alter themselves so that they can be more exciting, more keyed-up or more 'alive' people. Gradually, though, they can only feel alive, only feel 'themselves' when they are in the grip of their addiction. It seems to addicts that their fix, whatever it might be, puts them in touch with themselves, with the very core of their being. In fact, what is happening is the very opposite.

All addictions alienate us from ourselves, which is why any journey of personal growth must begin by separating ourselves from our addictions.

One of the overwhelming characteristics of an addiction is the denial that surrounds it. Before starting recovery, all addicts will tell you and, more importantly, tell themselves, that they could stop drinking, gambling, working hard or whatever, if they really wanted to, but that they enjoy drinking or gambling to excess. A compulsive eater will tell you – and will truly believe – that he or she does not eat any more than a thin person. When did a vastly overweight person admit to being a greedy glutton? It's the thin people who tell the world they are big eaters.

Research now indicates that the problem almost always starts with the family of origin. Addicts and codependents almost always come from families where one or both parents had been an active addict – and where this addiction was probably hidden or covered up. The point about addicts is that they cannot relate properly to other people, whether these people are casual acquaintances or their own spouses and children. And they certainly cannot relate properly to themselves. They don't know themselves, and so they cannot be true to themselves. Addicts are, essentially, people who don't know what 'me' is.

One of the best-known American writers on addiction, Anne Wilson Schaef, believes that, nowadays, the whole of society is addicted. We are all, she believes, dishonest, robotic and alienated from ourselves. And it is because we feel so uncomfortable with ourselves as we are that we stumble towards the nearest fix. For some, this will be alcohol. For others, food. For yet more people, sex, or romance addiction. Schaef believes that addictions, in large part, stem from the white male system under which we live, a system which, she believes, tries to be controlling, omnipotent, omniscient – and operates under the mistaken belief that people, nature, events and relationships can be rigidly controlled.

The problem is that maintaining an illustory system takes a great deal of stress, both mental and physical. Addictions are one way of trying to cope with this stress. Some people may say 'I need a drink'; others may take refuge in tranquillisers, cigarettes and cups of coffee, to calm and steady their nerves.

In an ideal society, we would not need these artificial fixes. But the more alienated from our true selves we become, the more we will need addictive substances. They are a desperate attempt to make ourselves feel all right, but they are fool's gold, leading us into a fool's paradise. Not that there is anything unintelligent about addictions – some of the world's greatest geniuses have also been hopeless addicts, for example Coleridge, Hemingway, Augustus John, Scott Fitzgerald to name but a few.

Because addictions have such a powerful hold, there is always a great deal of pain involved in releasing ourselves from their grip. I have already described how the most difficult thing in my own life was giving up smoking. I had to deal with all the feelings associated with addiction – shame, denial, low self-esteem, feelings of powerless, utter panic when my fix wasn't there, a complete inability to attend a social function or get on with my work without the fix in my fingers.

If giving up cigarettes is so difficult, how much more tough is releasing oneself from an addiction which powerfully alters consciousness, and which may have already made a person's life unliveable.

Yet, it is always worth it in the end because life on the other side is so much more wonderful than before. If ever I long for a cigarette, I ask myself: do I really want to go back to that dependency which gripped me with cold terror every time my supply threatened to run out? Do I really want to be in thrall to a weed which is expensive, destroys my health, makes me anti-social and annoys other people?

Of course not. The momentary pleasure associated with smoking a cigarette is completely outweighed by the negative, compulsive aspects. And the same is true of any addiction.

The 12-Step Programme

The 12-Step programme is, as we have said, by far the most effective way of dealing with any form of compulsive behaviour. It is of course very famous, although I am constantly surprised at the number of people who imagine it is something only for religious people. The 12-Step programme works just as well for atheists and agnostics as for believers, although many non-believers have stumbled over the 'God' aspect of the steps.

As so very many self-help groups use the 12-Step programme, or versions of it, I will briefly outline and explain it here. The Steps are, in fact, powerful messages for anybody serious about personal growth, because they encapsulate what living a good life is all about. Understanding the

Steps can help all of us to understand and identify aspects of our own behaviour which may be preventing us from getting to know ourselves properly. If Anne Wilson Schaef is right, we are *all* addicts – which is why we need so much help with our own personal growth.

So here are the Steps, as relevant now as when they were first formulated in the 1930s, during the Prohibition era in America. One of the best things about them is that you don't have to go on a highly expensive course to learn them. They are available, free, to anybody who is serious about their own personal growth.

And they form the cornerstone of all the many 'anonymous' self-help groups, such as Alcoholics Anonymous, Gamblers Anonymous, Narcotics Anonymous, Families Anonymous, Sex Addicts Anonymous, Overeaters Anonymous, Codependents Anonymous, Children of Alcoholics and so on. You can be sure that every single 'anonymous' recovery group will use these Steps, as do the various 'Minnesota Model' rehabilitation centres (see page 93).

Step 1

We admitted we were powerless over our addiction – that our lives had become unmanageable.

Explanation: Most addicts have the illusion that they are in control, that they can zap the addiction any time they like. This first step, often the most painful, allows people to admit that the addiction is actually controlling them, and that it is gradually taking away their conscious choice of action. Indeed, it may have already done so. The first step allows us to face up to and admit the reality of the addiction.

Step 2

Came to believe that a power greater than ourselves could restore us to sanity.

Explanation: Many people have difficulty with this step, as it sounds so Christian, handing over to God. But all it need mean here is that the power of the group, which is greater than ourselves, can be instrumental in helping us on the road to sobriety. Accepting this step means to acknowledge that help is needed, that it is actually impossible to recover completely on your own.

Step 3

Made a decision to turn our will and our lives over to the care of God as we understood God.

Explanation: Again, many people have stumbled over this step because it sounds religious. But this can mean that we are prepared to listen, at last, to the authentic voice within, rather than trying to override it all the time with reason, logic and the illusion of control. One of the greatest stumbling-blocks for addicts is this belief that they are in control, that they are logical, rational people. The more their lives go out of control, the more they believe they are in charge. In fact, the addiction is in charge – and all the addict's values, morals and ethics are governed by the compulsive behaviour.

Step 4

Made a searching and fearless moral inventory of ourselves.

Explanation: This does not mean that we should blame or castigate ourselves to make us feel far worse than we do already. All addicts are already coping with great shame and self-hatred. It means, rather, to come to terms with ourselves, to understand properly the dynamics of our actions, and to realise that low self-esteem, a wish to control and a desire to blame other people has led to our present position.

By taking this fourth step, we can come to know ourselves as we are, and learn to stop hiding from ourselves. Instead of trying to blame others or outside circumstances for our present situation, we can come to realise that we have created it through our own actions. Step 4 can be seen as the beginning of raised self-esteem and self-confidence.

Step 5

Admitted to God, to ourselves, and to another human being the exact nature of our wrongs.

Explanation: Basically, this step means to replace dishonesty, which has characterised all of our actions so far, with honesty. As dishonesty has become such a habit with all addicts, this step means admitting that we have not revealed ourselves, that we have tried to keep our true selves hidden, even from ourselves. We have deluded everybody, most of all ourselves, and recovery is impossible until this can be understood.

Step 6
Were entirely ready to have God remove all these defects of character.

Explanation: You don't have to believe in God to work this step. What this means is that we become willing to let go of all the dysfunctional habits which have prolonged our addiction, such as controlling and manipulating other people, worrying, blaming our misfortunes on others, fears, low self-esteem (not always understood as a character defect), self-neglect, self-rejection, hatred of the self and lack of trust in ourselves.

Step 7
Humbly asked God to remove our shortcomings.

Explanation: Many, if not most addicts, imagine that it is their character defects – their anger, aggression, attachment – which make them what they are, and if these were removed, there would be no individuality left. In fact, the opposite happens. With this step, we ask that all the defect should fall away, so that the genuine person underneath can emerge – the loving, authentically feeling, healthy, positive individual who is a joy to have around, and who can be happy, confident and at peace with him or herself.

Melody Beattie, author of the *Codependents' Guide to the Twelve Steps* (Piatkus) explains that 'humbly ask God' does not mean we have to pray to God to take these defects away, but that we acknowledge the help of a 'higher power'. Again, this can be interpreted as the power of the group, our own intuitive voice or an outside God, depending on your set of beliefs.

Step 8
Made a list of all persons we had harmed, and became willing to make amends to them all.

Explanation: All addicts, without exception, harm other people. Most of all, they harm themselves. Yet, most addicts sincerely believe that it's the other way round, that other people have harmed *them* – their bosses, their spouses, their parents, their lovers.

Yes, we have been harmed – yet the people who harmed us could not do anything other than they did. If they could have behaved better, they would have done. This step involves making a list of those we have used, been angry with, raged against, been dishonest with, shamed, felt uncomfortable with, owed money to. The idea of this step is to put paid to all the shame and guilt we feel in connection with these people, and wipe the slate clean so that it no longer preys on our mind.

Step 9
Made direct amends to such people wherever possible, except where to do so would injure them or others.

Explanation: Here, we acknowledge that other people are separate from ourselves, not extensions of ourselves, which is what all addicts believe. In this step we forgive all those people who may have treated us badly, and wipe out the score. It does not mean, as Melody Beattie points out, that we give permission to continue to treat us badly. In essence, this step shows us that we should detach from other people, not take responsibility for them, or continue to be bound to them by ties of hate, resentment or hostility.

We let them go – and heal ourselves in the process.

Step 10
Continue to take personal inventory and when we were wrong, promptly admitted it.

Explanation: This means that we acknowledge we have to continue to be honest, to understand our motives and to keep alert for when denial, shame, guilt or any self-destructive behaviours creep in, as they will do. Over the years of active addiction, these behaviours will have become an ingrained habit, so they must be carefully and continuously monitored.

Step 11
Sought through prayer and meditation to improve our conscious contact with God as we understood God, praying only for knowledge of God's will for us and the power to carry that out.

Explanation: Acknowledging the need for prayer and meditation means that we have to remember to allow ourselves periods of quiet to listen to that authentic voice inside, the voice of all knowledge and wisdom which is already embedded in us, but which has been stilled and silenced, and muffled through the years of addiction.

What the 12 Steps mean, above all, is that we ask God, our inner voice, whatever, to remove the *ego* and arrogance which has allowed us to continue in our addictive behaviour. Once we can remove these, we are well on the way to recovery. Ego means believing we are in control, it means a shutting-down of our emotions and genuine reactions. It is ego, lack of genuine humility, which keeps us addicted.

Step 12

Having had a spiritual awakening as a result of these steps, we tried to carry this message to others and to practise these principles in all our affairs.

Explanation: This means that we should not keep the message of hope, love and positivity to ourselves, but should, by our own example, let other people see that it is possible to become sober, to take responsibility, to make valid choices and free ourselves from the stranglehold of addictive behaviour.

The word 'spiritual' in this step bothers many people, as spirituality is for so many people intimately associated with religious observances which may, and indeed often are, just another kind of addiction. A 'spiritual awakening' means to become alive to the kind of people we really are – living, positive, intelligent, full of hope and optimism, and not carrying a burden of rage and anger around with us. It means we can spread light and love and happiness, instead of gloom and despair. We give out love instead of just trying to take it.

I will now outline the work of the main 'anonymous' organisations, then describe briefly a number of other self-help organisations which have been set up for people with specific difficulties such as bereavement, cancer, handicapped children. Finally I will give some ideas as to how to set up a self-help group, for those who feel so inclined.

(*Note*: Some people might wonder why all the self-help addiction recovery groups following the 12 Steps make such a feature of the 'anonymous' aspect. The reason is that the groups are dedicated to helping people overcome their addiction, and they feel that any identification may prevent this. Also, some members of the group might have been in prison, have broken the law or committed terrible crimes.

By allowing everybody to be anonymous, the group can focus entirely on the presenting problem, which is the addiction, without allowing anything else to get in the way. There is also the understanding that because of our addictions we are all exactly like the other members of the group, whatever our sex, social background, colour, educational or career attainments.)

Alcoholics Anonymous

This is by far the best-known type of help available for alcoholics throughout the world. There are around 1500 AA groups around the country, and AA describes itself as a 'fellowship of men and women who share their experiences, strength and hope with each other so that they may solve their common problem and help others to recover from alcoholism'. AA groups are for people who realise that they may need help to overcome their drinking problem, and who have accepted that their alcoholism has become unmanageable and destructive. AA accepts that alcoholism is a progressive disease – a definition not agreed with by every approach to drinking problems – but one which can be overcome by a genuine understanding of the problem.

To AA, alcoholics can never be considered 'cured' – they are always 'in recovery'.

It is easy enough to go to an AA meeting. You do not have to see a doctor or get any kind of referral. All you have to do is to look up the nearest branch of AA in your phone book, or write to the Head Office, and you will be put in touch with your nearest branch. Your identity will never be revealed, and you will be expected to honour all confidences among other members of the group. The Head Office can arrange for you to go to your first AA meeting, and they will tell you what to expect.

Although it may seem simple enough to pick up the phone or write a letter, in fact, as all acloholics know, admitting the problem and accepting that you may need help is a very big step. It is, actually, the first step on the road to recovery.

For information contact AA Head Office: General Services Office, Great Britain, PO Box 1, Stonebow House, York YO1 2NJ. Tel: 0904 644026.

London Regional Telephone Service: Tel: 071–352 3001.

Al-Anon

This is for family members who may have been affected by a relative's drinking. Al-Anon is for anybody who 'loves an alcoholic', and the main message of the fellowship meetings is to encourage the relative to try and stop controlling the alcoholic's behaviour, which in any case is fighting a losing battle. But, because this may not be fully recognised, there is support and guidance available from others who have been down this route themselves. Al-Anon encourages people to recognise that they can only ever control and change their own behaviour, and they are powerless over other people's habits and drinking. It is not possible for anybody else to rescue, reform or bully the alcoholic – this can only come from the alcoholic personally.

For further information contact: Head Office. Tel: 071–403 0888. Or look in your local telephone directory for your nearest branch. This is also the number for Alateen, the group for teenagers and young people who have been harmed by a parent's drinking.

Gamblers Anonymous

This works on exactly the same principle as Alcoholics Anonymous, except that it helps active gamblers to admit to and recover from their problem. The route to help, the fellowship aspect, is exactly the same as with AA.

GA can be contacted at: PO Box 88, London SW10 0EU. Tel: 081– 741 4181. **Alternatively**: 17/23 Blantyre Street, London SW10 0DT. Tel: 071–352 3060.

Other 'Anonymous' Organisations

Other well-known 'anonymous' organisations offering fellowship help, guidance and support include the following:

Families Anonymous (for the families and relatives of drug users): 650 Holloway Road, London N19 3NU. Tel: 071–281 8889.
Narcotics Anonymous (active drug users): UK Service Office, 79 Lots Road, London SW10. Tel: 071–351 6794.
Overeaters Anonymous: 081–981 9363.
Sex and Love Addicts Anonymous: The Recovery Trust, PO Box BM 3157, London WC1N 3XX. This, one of the latest addiction self-help groups to arrive in the UK from America, helps people to identify and cope with sex and romance addiction which is not being recognised as being a disease as powerful and destructive, in its own way, as alcoholism or gambling. Fellowship members can work towards 'sobriety' in this as much as with any other form of addiction.

The newer organisations based on the same 12-Step programme, *National Association for Children of Alcoholics* and the *Codependents Anonymous*, are perhaps less well known than the above, but have come into being to address the enormous problems faced by people who have grown up in alcoholic, addicted or otherwise severely dysfunctional homes, and who need a great deal of help to address and overcome these painful, long-denied difficulties. Already, these groups are becoming a lifeline for those who know they have severe difficulties with relating to other people and getting their own needs met, but who may not be fully aware of why or how these problems were caused.

Children of Alcoholics

Although AA has been going for more than 60 years, it has only been realised relatively recently that children of alcoholic families can suffer as much as, if not even more than, the active alcoholic. At least the alcoholic can find some release and comfort in drink. The child, who is at the mercy of the adults, can find no such outlet.

Research on children of alcoholics has shown that these people, however old they are, can never really grow up. Also, because they have usually denied their own problems, or pretended that their own families were perfect, they risk passing on the same problems to the next generation, their own children. Thus the difficulties reverberate down the generations.

The play *Long Day's Journey into Night*, by Eugene O'Neill, exactly captures the archetypal dysfunctional family, where the parents' addiction problems are passed down to the children, and nobody can have a proper relationship with anybody else.

There are now a number of agencies which can help children of alcoholics to recognise and deal with the problems created by growing up in an alcoholic home.

Adult Children of Alcoholics: The Information Officer, 33 Upper Whistler Walk, London SW10 0ER. Tel: 071–376 5205.

The National Association for the Children of Alcoholics: PO Box 64, Fishponds, Bristol BS16 2UE. Tel: 0800 289 0611/0272 573432.

St Joseph's Centre for Addiction: Holy Cross Hospital, Hindhead Road, Haslemere, Surrey GU27 1NQ. Tel: 0428 656517. This is a professional therapy unit, but they can put you in touch with relevant self-help groups if you like.

Codependents Anonymous

'Codependency' is a term that is already widely used in America, but so far it has been quite strongly resisted in Britain and the rest of Europe, partly because it seems to be difficult to understand and partly because it appears to be yet another of those 'American' problems which we can do well without. But to my mind the whole concept of codependency (in many ways an unsatisfactory word, but it has now passed into the language so we have to accept it), has shed so much valuable light on why so very many people appear to be unable to form proper relationships, are never happy with their lives and are always yearning for something they haven't got, that we can't just ignore it any longer.

While we remain codependent, that is, while we attach ourselves needily to other people, we can never attain any genuine measure of personal growth, because it means we are reacting rather than acting. It has been established that codependency starts in childhood, when we begin to feel responsible for our parents rather than the other way round, and that it is intimately related to alcoholism or other serious family dysfunction.

The reason there are two separate self-help organisations, one for children of alcoholics and another for codependents, is because not all codependents come from alcoholic backgrounds, so might not so easily identify with the problem.

In a sense, we are all codependents. We become raging codependents when 'hell is other people' in Sartre's words. We cannot escape from their demands; they seem to need us all the time, or we seem to need them – yet none of this needing and attachment makes us happy. It just makes us despair, and become full of resentment and hostility.

Codependents essentially are people who have very little sense of their own identity, and so take refuge in playing stereotyped roles – the kindly doctor, the overworked, caring politician, the nurturing mother – rather than being truly themselves. They are people who need to be needed, and confuse being needed with being wanted. The usual explanation is that codependency has its origin in families where parents were simply not there for their children, so the children never grew up with a proper sense of self, or genuine inner confidence.

For codependents, the substance of addiction is other people. They love nothing more than to feel needed and wanted, and they find it hard to say no and to assert themselves properly. They are people who need people, but they are emphatically not the happiest people in the world. Instead, they are miserable and confused. They confuse being needed with genuine love, and often try to bind people to them. Overwhelmingly, codependents try to control other people – mainly because they feel they cannot control themselves. Controlling others seems easier. A codependent is somebody who says: 'I'd be all right if only everybody else would change.'

The main reason codependents latch on to others in such a way is because they don't know who they are themselves; they have no strong sense of identity. They feel empty inside. CodA groups help people who have identified themselves as codependents to understand the processes whereby they came to their present plight, and to learn to love themselves, to be their own 'parent' – as often, their own parents were missing or absent in any real sense – and to become assertive, to define their own needs and take responsibility for themselves, instead of always taking care of other people.

Information from: Codependents Anonymous, PO Box 1292, London N4 2XX. Tel: 071–409 0029.

The Minnesota Model

I've included this here, even though it is not strictly self-help, as it is intimately based on the 12-Step programme. The Minnesota Model, which usually takes place in a residential rehabilitation centre and consists of group therapy, is always administered by people who have 'been there'. All the group leaders are in recovery themselves.

This is where the concept of 'tough love' comes in, and the Model works equally well for any type of serious addiction such as gambling, alcoholism, eating disorders (overeating, anorexia, bulimia), codependency and illicit drug use. The idea is that it is wrong to try and bale out an addict, to cover up for them, but that the only way an addict can ever recover is to have the opportunity to face up to the consequences of their own behaviour. Thus, in a Minnesota Model centre, a drug user caught using would be expelled instantly, an overeater buying a Mars Bar would find herself out on the streets.

As one group leader put it: 'This is the only prison where you are turned out for bad behaviour!'

People usually reach these rehabilitation centres – which are extremely expensive (at twice the price of Eton) even though all are charities and non profit-making – when they have reached the end of their tether, when they have reached their own personal rock bottom. Mostly, people stay for six weeks, and attend twice-daily group therapy courses. The aim is complete sobriety from their particular drug except, of course, for overeaters, who must henceforth abstain from white flour and sugar, as these are seen as the foods with greatest addiction potential.

The Promis Recovery Centre, which uses the Minnesota Model, is at: The Old Court House, Pinners Hill, Nonnington, Kent CT14 4LL. Tel: 0304 841700. Also, St Joseph's Centre, address as above.

Other Self-Help and Support Groups

Many groups have been formed to help people deal with a particular problem in their life, or to gain power through numbers, rather than being specifically for personal growth. However, when a group of people band together for a specific self-help cause, growth is very often the result, even though it may not have been the initial impetus.

One of the earliest self-help groups in the UK was the Hyperactive Children's Support Group, started by one young mother, Sally Bunday, whose child Miles appeared to be hyperactive. Although little was known about the condition at the time, and doctors tended to dismiss it as middle-class parents trying to find a smart way of describing bad behaviour, the group persisted, and hyperactivity is now recognised as a definite condition, allied to allergy, which affects some children, and which has nothing to do with deliberate naughtiness.

So, through setting up their own support group, many ordinary, previously powerless women and men became well-informed, assertive and confident.

A similar success story was the National Association for Premenstrual Syndrome, formed at a time when PMS was very little recognised, and was seen as a weakness, a potent reason why women should not have positions of power and influence – their hormones would always be liable to play them up. But, through NAPS and similar organisations, it has been realised that PMS is a condition which can be treated and overcome – not a monthly misery which just has to be endured.

Other people who have campaigned and made names for themselves for starting self-help groups to bring ignored or hidden conditions to public notice are Angela Kilmartin, who started a group for sufferers of cystitis and thrush, and Joan Jerome, who began a self-help group for tranquilliser users after recovering from her own twenty-year addiction to the pills.

There are now self-help and support groups for almost every problem that exists, from incest and child abuse, to abortion, infertility, AIDS, bereavement, for parents of crying babies, and for almost every serious and chronic illness. The modern advice is: don't take what 'experts' tell you as gospel – but join a suitable self-help group – or form one yourself. Then you can meet other people in exactly the same position as yourself, and through networking and pooling ideas, you can work out ways of treating or overcoming the problems you face.

Information: To find out whether there is a suitable self-help group for your needs, you can contact your local Citizens' Advice Bureau or local library. The National Self-Help Support Centre, National Council for Voluntary Organisations, 26 Bedford Square, London WC1B 3HU, has an extensive list.

Starting Your Own Self-Help Group

All the self-help groups which have become well known and successful were the result of the inspiration of just one person, or possibly a small group of people. So, if there is not yet a group which meets your specific requirements, why not start one up? The National Self-Help Support Centre, address above, provides help for people who wish to do this, and can direct you to agencies giving more specific guidance.

The first thing you must do is to contact potential members. This is best done by notices in public places, or by contacting local radio helplines. Decide whether you want your home address and telephone number given out, or whether you would rather work through a box or BM (British Monomark) number.

You will also have to decide whether you are prepared for people to meet in your home, or whether you want to rent premises. At each stage, finances will have to be taken into account. Premises and advertising cost money. Letters to newspapers cost nothing, and often do the trick. The National Housewives' Register, for instance, which evolved into a thriving national organisation, began when Maureen Nicol wrote an anguished letter to *The Guardian* in 1960.

And the Noise Abatement Society started life when John Connell, a Kent businessman, wrote about noise in a letter to *The Daily Telegraph* – and was astonished to get 4000 replies.

Then you will have to decide how the group is to be run, and what it is to achieve. Are you campaigning to change the law? To empower individuals? To meet and discuss specific ways of overcoming a common problem, such as PMS or cystitis? Will the group be confidential, or are the meetings to be 'open'? Are members' names to be circulated, or kept secret?

Here, the National Centre can help to start you off, if you are unsure. Over the years, the self-help movement has worked out its own effective ways of operating, and you might well have the input of people who are used to setting up and running such groups.

Many groups, of course, evolve out of trial and error, but you will need to be clear as to whether they are mainly for therapeutic reasons, to provide a forum for an exchange of ideas, a listening service for people in trouble, or whatever. Also, don't forget that the work of organising the group will probably devolve on one person: do you want to take that responsibility, or should it be shared?

Should members have a definite commitment – or just turn up if they feel like it? The Laughter Clinic in Birmingham, for example, although not exactly self-help, as it is run by therapist Robert Holden, is a drop-in clinic. This means that the numbers can vary greatly, also that there is no commitment to attending. There are, of course, pros and cons with each approach, and you have to decide which one suits the kind of self-help group you are envisaging.

Other aspects to consider are: will members of the group touch and hug, as happens in co-counselling? Will you meet socially, or only as part of the group? How formal or informal do you want it to be, i.e. will there be minutes, subscriptions, secretaries, treasurers – or not? If not, thought has to be given to how the group will be financed to meet expenses such as mailing, flyers, advertising, leaflets.

Then, how is the group to be run? Will you have a formal agenda, a topic for each session or will you just see how it goes? Will you meet once a week, once a month, every night? 12-Step programmes, for example, commonly meet every night, as this amount of commitment is considered part of the recovery itself.

Setting up and running a self-help group will enable you to realise that you are not alone in your problem, whatever it might be. If attending a self-help group is empowering, think what starting one can do!

Angela Kilmartin, who started the U and I Club (now disbanded) for cystitis sufferers, is an attractive and highly confident woman in her early fifties. She has a brisk, no-nonsense manner, and is a semi-professional singer. When she first married, and realised she had an illness which was never talked about, she was quite a different person. She said:

'*I never imagined at the outset that speaking out about my agony and starting the first self-help club for cystitis sufferers would have made me a world-wide expert on the subject, in demand for conferences and lectures everywhere. I had just got married, and knew nothing whatever.*

'*Because of cystitis, my honeymoon was sheer agony, and the subject was never even mentioned in those days. Doctors knew little about it and, immediately before my generation, women died. Antibiotics now meant that we didn't die, but we still suffered.*

'*I had to start from scratch, and discover for myself which measures worked. I found that, most of all, cystitis sufferers could help themselves by following a few simple hygiene rules. I wrote books, I started to lecture, I divorced my husband, I became financially self-sufficient – all because I took my fate into my own hands, and didn't just rely on doctors.*

'*When you start a self-help group, you don't just wait for "them" to do something – you do it yourself.*'

Women's Groups

Women's groups have undoubtedly been a catalyst for major change in our society. In their present form, they started with consciousness-raising groups in America, where women could get together and talk over what was troubling them. They started initially mainly as a result of Betty Friedan's book *The Feminine Mystique*.

Never highly organised or a national network, women's groups were always somewhat informal and fragile, with groups often disbanding after a few weeks. However, groups are always being reformed, and the 'problem that has no name' as Betty Friedan termed it, is still with us.

Consciousness-raising, or CR groups, led to groups of women meeting to discuss their health, their bodies, to learn about themselves by talking and by self-examination, to pool ideas, doubts and fears, to mention things they had never dared raise with another human being before. CR groups provided a powerful kind of 'talking cure' where women could talk through their problems, find that other women thought exactly the same, and try to work out solutions so that they could live their lives more effectively.

CR groups are still going, but as ever, they are not well organised and tend to consist of small pockets of women who meet, either in each other's houses, or in local halls, once a month or so. They can be found by looking at notices in public places, through feminist magazines, in church porches, through Citizens' Advice Bureaux, newsagents' windows, local newspapers and so on. They can be a good, non-threatening and inexpensive start on the road to self-discovery for a woman who feels isolated and unhappy, without perhaps knowing why.

For instance, *Julia* secretly joined a women's group in her area when her marriage was going through terrible difficulties. She and her husband had been to marriage guidance counselling, but this did not seem to be providing any answers. She realised that her husband would strongly object if he knew she was going to meetings run by 'hairy-legged bra-burners' but she went nevertheless – and found the meetings an absolute revelation.

She said:

'I had always thought that the reason my marriage wasn't working was because there was something wrong with me. Through talking to the other women, though, I realised that my problems weren't unique to me but were shared by everybody in the group. All of us in the group, without exception, had thought that the thing to do was to get married, have children and put other people first, perhaps trying to fit in a little part-time job at the same time.

'None of us were career high flyers, which was a relief to me, as I might have felt overawed. We were all ordinary women facing a crisis. We wondered why everything seemed to have gone wrong. I met every month with the group for a year – there were about eight of us – before making the decision to leave my husband and branch out on my own. The marriage was slowly killing me – not because my husband was a horrible person, because he wasn't – but because I had compromised so much over the years so that I no longer knew who I was. After years in the home, my self-confidence had evaporated to the point where it was more or less non-existent, and I could hardly even buy a train ticket on my own, let alone go to the cinema, a restaurant or theatre by myself.

'Now, thanks to the initial consciousness-raising provided by the group, I have left my husband, and am living on my own, having the best time of my life. Never have I been so happy, because for the first time ever, I'm doing what's right for me.'

Julia feels that local women's groups can give confidence to women who want to take the first steps to freedom, but have lost confidence in how to go about it. She stresses that divorce or separation is not the inevitable outcome – she is the only one in her group so far to have got divorced. But the thing about the group, she says, is that it helped her to open her eyes to how she had been limiting herself over the years.

She added:

'It can be very painful to realise that the choices you made may not have benefited you at all, to admit this, and to see what to do for the future. Through the group, I had to ask myself some very uncomfortable questions, and it wasn't until I found the answers within myself that I gained the courage to lead my own life.

*As with many other women, I had been brought up to please others, condi-
tioned to think that my place in the world was secondary, and that a
husband would support and look after me. All those things, I realised later,
were illusions – and they weren't doing me any good at all.'*

During the 1980s, women's groups tended to disappear as many
women felt that the fight was now over, and the need for separatist groups
was gone. Now, they are coming back as it is being realised that we still
need to band together and make sure that the gains we fought for all those
years ago don't disappear.

Women Unlimited has been set up to offer a whole range of courses
and therapy groups to women. There are many therapies on offer at the
Centre, including time and stress management, individual and group
counselling, and empowerment workshops.

Information from: Women Unlimited, 79 Pathfield Road, London
SW16 5PA. Tel: 081–677 7503.

Goddess Groups

Consciousness-raising groups may not appeal to some women. Those
who feel that such groups are not for them may be interested in the newer
Goddess movement, which encourages women to hark back to an earlier
age when female principles, symbolised in the ancient goddesses, were
the more important ones. Goddess groups are more esoteric and spiritual
than CR groups, and to some extent challenge the Darwinian idea that we
are always evolving and improving.

The 'emerging woman' and the 'emerging female system' are very
much part and parcel of present-day personal growth. They are concepts
for personal and planetary change, so that we can not just claim our own
power, but realise that the hierarchical male model may not be a good
blueprint for the future.

Unlike CR groups, which came directly out of the feminist movements
of the 1970s, the goddess idea harks back to all ancient cultures – Eastern,
American Indian, tribal. Understanding the goddess archetypes can,
according to those who have benefited from this knowledge, help us each
to know exactly what sort of person we might be – and act accordingly.

For instance, there is no point in trying to be an earth mother if you are a hunter, go-getter type. There are now a number of astrologers specialising in goddess revelations, so if you want to know which type you are, why not go and find out? It may help you to get to know and reclaim the power that you may temporarily have lost by trying to be somebody you are not.

Modern goddess lore has been taken mainly from the Greek goddesses. Here is a brief description of the main archetypes:

Artemis, *Athena* and *Hestia* are the self-contained goddesses, women who do not necessarily need a partner, and who absolutely have to be their own person. It is probably a mistake for these types to imagine they can settle down happily as wives and mothers, or take a supporting role in somebody else's life.

The *Artemis* type (goddess of hunting) is independent, loves solitude and will probably find her primary relationships with other women. *Athena* is a spokeswoman type, out in front, fearless and independent. Modern Athena women include Margaret Thatcher, Indira Gandhi and Shirley Maclaine. *Hestia*, goddess of the hearth, is kind, thoughtful and content, not interested in being a public figure.

Now we come on to some very different types. The *Hera* figure is committed, often to her husband or partner, and fiercely loyal. She needs to be in a relationship to feel complete, and does not function well on her own. She tends to be a Mrs and does not believe that marriage is a subjugation. *Demeter*, the earth goddess, had to recover her lost daughter Persephone from the underworld. She is characterised as a helping type of woman, maybe a nurse or doctor, social worker or midwife. She may suffer greatly from the 'empty nest' syndrome.

Persephone, Demeter's daughter, is innocent, charming, vulnerable and often very attractive to men. She may seem naïve, a 'little girl' type, insecure and afraid of the outside world. She is the type of woman who could easily form dysfunctional relationships.

Aphrodite, the goddess of love, is magnetic, alluring, feminine and romantic. She tends to be a matchmaker and often goes through very many relationships herself. But always, she sees herself in a relationship, never on her own.

The strength of the goddess concept is that it allows us to realise that we are all different, and that what suits one person may be quite wrong for another. As with other aspects of personal growth, an appreciation of the goddess archetypes can help us to start to listen to that voice within, the voice that is always in danger of being silenced by the world around us.

Women who are interested in exploring the meaning of the goddess archetypes can contact Isis, which holds a number of workshops and groups to discuss how the ancient goddess ideas can be incorporated into modern life. There are also counselling and therapy sessions.

Information from: Isis, 33 Lorn Road, London SW9 0AB. Tel: 071–733 7883.

(*Note*: Women Unlimited and Isis are not self-help groups, but are useful for women who wish to explore further the ideas discussed in this section.)

Men's Groups

In most areas of life, it seems as if women have been overshadowed by men. In the area of self-help and therapy groups, however, it's the other way round.

In many ways, the history of our times has been that of groups of men getting together, from the medieval guilds, to freemasons, men's clubs and societies, most of which excluded women.

So why are consciousness-raising men's groups growing in popularity? The answer is simply because it is increasingly being realised that a system which does not benefit half of the human race – the dominant white male system – is hardly going to benefit the other half. As the poet Shelley wrote: 'If woman is a slave, can man be free?'

One of the key books for the men's movement has been *Iron John*, by Robert Bly (Element) which encourages men to look at ancient traditions of male initiation, so that they can have mentors of their own sex to initiate them into genuine masculinity. All too often, in modern life, the father-figure has been absent or remote, providing no proper role model or any chance of a real relationship. Boys are brought up mainly by women. As Bly, and increasingly, psychologists, are beginning to see it, when boys are brought up mainly by women they both lose sight of the 'inner man' and also are in danger of developing a dangerous 'tough guy' persona which tends to see women as inferior creatures.

Boys cannot imitate women, so they strive to be different – and superior. On the whole, the current men's movement is one that looks again at parenthood, at the part that fathers should be playing in bringing up their children. In the past, they have, on the whole, abdicated this role.

There are two main types of men's groups, just as there are two distinct types of women's groups: one is practical, and the other is more esoteric, harking back to ancient wisdoms and initiations, as with the Goddess Movement for women.

The practical men's groups, such as Fathers Need Families, are for men, who are, for one reason or another, separated from their families through divorce or separation. In most instances, it is the mother who gains custody of the children, and fathers frequently never see their families again. There are now several pressure groups to try and even up the score, as absent fathers see it.

There are now a number of men's groups meeting regularly, sending out newsletters and information to members so that men can join forces in redressing what they see as a monstrous imbalance. There are now many men who feel that feminism has gone too far, and that fathers, particularly, have been forced on to the sidelines.

The more esoteric men's groups also focus on the way that fathers no longer seem to take an active part in their sons' upbringing, but these groups hark back to ancient traditions, to try and see what has gone wrong, and how it can be put right, rather than invoking the law or ideas of justice to give fathers a fair deal.

As with the Goddess groups, these men's groups have the aim of helping men to get back in touch with deeper aspects of themselves, their emotions, their doubts and fears, so that they too can gain true self-confidence and self-respect. For very many men, the 'Iron John' approach may sound impossibly New Agey and alternative, but it marks a dramatic difference of approach from the old-style men's groups and clubs, which banded together mainly to increase and aggrandise male professional power at the expense of other people lower down the line.

In the past, most men's groups and clubs have tried to be exclusive in this way. For instance, smart London clubs excluded women and insisted on high membership fees so that they could remain exclusive and keep the riff-raff out. Now, of course, most are having to open their doors to women as male membership is tailing off in the recession and many cannot afford to keep going otherwise. Many golf clubs also excluded women, and certain ethnic groups – now they too are having to admit all comers.

The down side of all this is that there are ever-fewer places where men can meet on their own and talk by themselves. Younger men, particularly, are feeling a need to share their emotional experiences with other men, as they too are becoming isolated in nuclear families, living away from the places where they grew up, and are finding it difficult to establish firm male friendships.

The new message is that men and women need to band together on occasion, not to discuss or exclude the 'enemy', but in order to have an opportunity to discuss their deepest fears and problems in ways that only other members of the same sex will understand. The idea is that this new knowledge, information and insight can help people to relate in better ways to the opposite sex. Modern men's and women's groups operate on the basic truth that truly intimate and meaningful relationship are impossible until we first come to know ourselves and what we want.

In the past, men have often felt it was rather wimpish to join a group where problems and emotions could be discussed, but now, those days are drawing to a close. Men are realising, as well as women, that it actually takes a lot of courage and honesty to face up to and admit what the problem might be, and where they can usefully go from that point.

At the very least, joining a men's group to discuss important issues concerning deepest feelings has got to be better than sitting watching television or downing pints in the pub. But the 'stiff upper lip' mentality dies hard, so fiercely has it been instilled into so many men in the past. It can still seem that to open our hearts is a sign of weakness.

Information about men's groups from: National Men's Network, PO Box 154, Oxford OS2 9XJ.

Brothers is a group offering workshops and courses for men on such subjects as child development, sexuality and becoming a true man. Counselling and psychotherapy are also available. **Information from**: 207 Waller Road, London SE14 5LX. Tel: 071–639 9732.

Man to Man runs men's groups, both in the evenings and at weekends, to help men get in touch with their true emotions, and discover who they really are. **Information from**: 17 Mackeson Road, London NW3 2LU. Tel: 071–482 3588.

Also: *Fathers Need Families*, BM families, London WC1N 3XX. Tel: 081–866 0970.

Sweat Lodges

This is an idea from native America, which is gradually becoming popular for people who wish to expand their consciousness. What happens is that a group of men and women sit round a fire, and then crawl into the sweat lodge, which is like a primitive sauna, built from wood and twigs, with sleeping bags inside. It is pitch black, with no lighting, and completely sealed off from the elements. Sweat lodge ceremonies take place in the dead of night.

A shaman – a priest and healer – tells the assembled group that they are entering the sweat lodge in order to be reborn. When everybody is in place, hot rocks are put in the centre of the lodge, so that there is intense heat. Every now and again, more sizzling rocks are brought in as the group is directed to pray to their guardian spirit, which might be an ancestor, Jesus, their higher power or whatever they choose.

As the ceremony proceeds, sweat starts to drip off everybody and there is extreme physical discomfort. Participants start to lose their sense of time, and become disorientated. It is at this stage that long-buried feelings, emotions and thoughts come to the surface – they are literally sweated out. People may start to groan and cry, or wail when they cannot bottle things up any longer, and all defences are down.

Eventually, when people imagine that any minute they will die from the heat and the agony of coping with their emotions rising up, the shaman – or person in charge of the ceremony – lifts back the entrance of the lodge, and lets the night air in. Those who have attended sweat lodge ceremonies say that after the process is over, they feel purified, as if all their mental and physical toxins have come out. The 'rebirth' that takes place is an opportunity for participants to get to know every aspect of themselves.

Information from: New Life Designs, Arnica House, 170 Campden Hill Road, London W8 7AS, tel: 071–938 3788 who can put you in touch with groups that organise sweat lodge ceremonies in the UK.

Co-Counselling

Co-counselling, also known as re-evaluation counselling, is a form of self-help psychotherapy, where the same two people take it in turns to be both counsellor and client. It is the ultimate form of non-authoritarian counselling, and now has a world-wide network.

The idea behind co-counselling is that the best person to help some-body in trouble is somebody else in trouble. Would-be co-counsellors must first attend a 'fundamentals' course, where the elements of the system are explained, and they are then introduced to a whole network of other people with whom they can be both counsellor and counselled.

In its simplest terms, co-counselling is like talking to a friend, except that the relationship will be detached, and the 'friend' will have learned how to listen in an empathic and non-judgemental way – something real friends don't always do. Touching and hugging are encouraged in co-counselling, but the relationship is supposed to be non-sexual and non-intimate.

It is intended for all people who wish to be more effective in their everyday lives, and is suitable for anybody who wishes to gain greater self-understanding and a sense of purpose in their lives.

The concept behind co-counselling is that basically we are all loving, enthusiastic, positive, intelligent people, but that over the years, layers of negativity and wrong ideas about ourselves, often instilled by others as we were growing up, will be working to hold us back. Early distress, according to the co-counselling philosophy, is the main reason why we are less effective than we could be.

Many of us also have learned to distrust other people, to imagine they are getting at us and want to do us down. The co-counselling relationship is intended to bring back a sense of trust and enable us to break down the inhibitions we may have concerning ourselves and our relationship with other people.

At the heart of the co-counselling message is the concept that it's not enough simply to acknowledge and remember early distress: in order to remove it, we have to discharge it. There is often a lot of emotion released in co-counselling sessions, and people can find it painful to discharge early hurts and deeply-buried emotions which may have been held in their systems for many years.

Overt signs of emotion, such as crying, trembling and raging, are encouraged as they are seen as a potent way of discharging old, negative and inappropriate feelings. What may have helped us to survive in the past is most probably stopping us from achieving our maximum enjoyment and fulfilment of life now, according to the co-counselling philosophy.

Once negative emotions and the baggage of the past have been discharged, then the basically loving, co-operative, trustful person can emerge.

It is because such discharge can be very difficult both for the counsellor and client to handle, that the introductory course is seen to be essential before embarking on this self-help therapy.

It is only when negativity has been discharged, and old self-sabotaging patterns reversed, that people can become effective at looking after themselves, learn to love themselves, and also learn to love and trust each other.

It is increasingly being realised that we are only 'as sick as our secret', and that when our secrets can be admitted and brought out into the open we can move forward into the future with confidence.

The growth of self-help groups, including co-counselling, has been instrumental in providing safe places, and safe people, for secrets to be shared and shed.

Genuine growth can take place only when we no longer need to hide secrets from ourselves. And self-help groups can be a major step on the way to discovering just what secrets we may be holding – we don't always know at first.

This is why co-counselling can be a good start for those who have not yet identified the secrets, the addictions, the self-sabotaging patterns, which are holding them back and preventing them from enjoying life to the full.

Further information about co-counselling from: Co-counselling, 17 Lisburen Road, London NW3 2NS. Tel: 071–485 0005.

Another contact is The London Co-counselling Community, 23 Bridge Avenue Mansions, London W6 9JB. Tel: 081–748 1407. Fundamentals training courses.

(*Note*: Some co-counselling training courses are free, others are not, but all are based on ability to pay, and none are expensive. Fees for the training courses (in 1993) vary from £40–£80.)

Chapter 5

Spiritual Organisations

Introduction

In many ways, the human potential movement and the upsurge of the spiritual movement have much in common. Both are concerned to help individuals maximise their potential, and replace negativity, low confidence and low self-esteem with positivity, greater self-assurance and a purposeful outlook on life. It is significant that many spiritual organisations which have established themselves since the 1960s are now holding 'positive thinking', healthy eating and lifestyle courses, as well as continuing their more mainstream spiritual work.

Although we live in an intensely materialistic age, spiritual organisations are not only mushrooming, but flourishing as never before. Many churches may be nearly empty on Sundays, but some of the more exotic spiritual movements have packed audiences at their seminars and gatherings. Those which have undoubtedly had the greatest impact are the Eastern-based movements which arrived in the West during the middle of this century, and whose teachings are inspired by ancient Hindu or Buddhist doctrines, rather than the more recent Judao-Christian beliefs.

Many people have found these organisations a gateway to personal growth and development, and an understanding of their own spirituality. For many people, the word 'spirituality' has pretty much the same effect as the word 'culture' was supposed to have on the Nazi leader Herman

Goering. But all it means in essence is an ability to get to the spirit, the pure essence, of ourselves, and realise ourselves as we truly are.

A self-realised being is somebody with supreme self-confidence and self-esteem, but with total lack of ego. Such a being is somebody who has a purpose in life, who can connect to all living things, who can look on other people with unconditional love but with detachment and respect. A fully realised individual does not seek after material, sensual pleasures or worldly fame, but has gained immense strength by being able to get in touch with their innermost being.

A spiritual person is not somebody who is impossibly holy, but who has faced his or her own personal demons, and is working to overcome them, to learn positive lessons from all experiences, to take responsibility for all actions, and who attempts to set only good actions and thoughts in motion. There are few, if any, people living in the world today who have attained this kind of perfection, but a genuine spiritual path will help on the way.

True spirituality has nothing to do with wearing special robes, chanting God's name, attending church, preaching or trying to repress sinful desires. It is, rather, a state of not having any desires for oneself, of being always calm and in control, and of not being at the mercy of negative emotions. You can be genuinely spiritual without ever going near a church or place of worship and, conversely, go to church, synagogue or mosque several times a week without ever understanding what spirituality is all about.

But why is it that we in the West have, to a large extent, forsaken our established religions and embraced the Eastern-based movements – for which in the West we have no tradition – with such enthusiasm?

I think one reason is that, although there is a yawning spiritual hunger in most people, one which, in the absence of anything else, tends to be filled either by the acquisition of material objects or with addictions, this has not been met by what most people see as traditional Christianity – moralistic, hierarchical and with increasingly little meaning or significance for people today.

Another reason is that established religions have political and nationalistic overtones. The Eastern-based movements which have become popular in the West have no such associations. They seem almost to have arrived from another planet, and are not connected to our class, national or social structure. They are outside of it, at least for Westerners.

True, there are upsurges of fundamentalist Christian belief, but on the whole these have not been major movements, nor have they been influential in a general sense. The meditation movements, by contrast, have affected our thinking in all kinds of ways, from stress management, to cancer and heart treatment, to business life.

With their chanting, their meditation, their promise of giving a complete experience, the Eastern movements have attracted and seduced many thousands of people who previously would have considered themselves either agnostics or outright atheists.

The essence of spiritual movements which foster personal growth is that they are non-political, non-nationalistic and offer an individual path for everybody. Also, although many people have found that nothing whatever happens during prayer, they have discovered that meditation often offers a very intense experience which can be so blissful that there is simply nothing to compare with it. A sense of super-consciousness, of meaningful insights, of being filled with peace and love, is commonly found during meditation sessions.

Transcendental Sex

A potent attraction of spiritual paths in the early days of the human potential movement was that they combined ancient spirituality and modern psychology with the opportunity to have transcendental sexual experiences. The best-known 'sex guru' of the 1970s was undoubtedly Bhagwan Shree Rajneesh, who taught that spirituality and sexuality were compatible, and that sex could be the gateway to intense spirituality and self-realisation.

It was a revelation for literally thousands of Westerners, particularly those who had been brought up to believe that sex was basically wrong and sinful, and who now, in the new permissive mode of the late 1960s, were learning a new approach. The chance to combine spirituality and sexuality was, for very many, irresistible.

Another guru who attracted an enormous following during the 1970s was Swami Muktananda, who brought Siddha Yoga over from the East. Both Bhagwan Shree Rajneesh and Swami Muktananda, who saw themselves as enlightened beings preaching a brand-new message to both East and West, attracted thousands of adoring followers and carved out for themselves highly luxurious lifestyles, driving around in Rolls-Royces and Cadillacs, staying at the best hotels, coining in money from their devotees, seminars, workshops and the literature they disseminated.

It should not be imagined either, that the early followers of these two charismatic gurus were displaced persons, or drop-outs who had lost their way and were eagerly clutching at any straws. From the first, these meditation movements attracted highly educated, rich, successful Westerners, professional people who felt that here was a brand-new message, something which could help them to get to know themselves better, as well as providing an exotic and different experience.

Transcendental Meditation

Some Eastern-based movements were specially tailored to suit the West. The best known of these was TM, or transcendental meditation, developed by the Maharishi Mahesh Yogi. Although the technique of meditating for twenty minutes twice a day on a personal mantra sounded strange when it first arrived over here, it has now become incorporated into holistic health programmes, and counselling for cancer, AIDS, heart disease and other serious illnesses now usually includes a meditation component.

The Maharishi can be credited with introducing meditation to the West. This has had such success that it is now used extensively in relaxation programmes for businesspeople, for those under stress and for those who have to work under high pressure. Meditation is now no longer seen as a strange Eastern practice, but a very effective way of stilling the 'traffic' in one's head, and clearing the mind of negative and unhelpful junk.

The attraction of TM is that it concentrates on the practical value of meditation and there is little emphasis on the root of Hindu teachings, such as reincarnation and karma. TM was seen very much as a practical tool for coping with stress in the modern world and, since its early days, it has gone from strength to strength, becoming a respected world-wide movement.

In the UK, TM has now entered the political arena, and fielded several hundred candidates in the 1992 general election, all of whom, it must be said, lost their deposits.

Other Movements

Another movement which has attracted a lot of attention and a large following, many from the world of showbusiness, is that of the Hare

Krishnas, or International Society for Krishna Consciousness. These are the people who wear orange robes and chant in Britain's high streets. They also have temples where people can get free vegetarian meals.

Sai Baba is an Indian guru who also has a very large following in the West. He is the man who is supposed to be able to materialise watches and other precious objects, although in recent years he seems to have concentrated more on producing holy ash, or vibuti (much more boring!). Psychologists and researchers have closely studied Sai Baba to see if they can detect any sleight of hand, and so far they have not been able to, although it must be said that he has not allowed any controlled trials of his work to be undertaken.

Two other Hindu-based spiritual movements which have become enormously successful and popular in the West are the Sivananda Yoga Vedanta Centres, and the Brahma Kumaris World Spiritual University. The Sivananda Yoga Centres, in common with the Hare Krishnas, teach directly from the Bhagavad-Gita. They teach hatha yoga and also hold many meditation intensives, fasting weekends, holiday retreats and other attractions for the Westerner. Asians also belong to these movements, of course – by no means all are aimed exclusively at the West.

The Brahma Kumaris are rather different from the others in that, although like the other Eastern-based movements they were founded by a man, the organisation is now headed exclusively by women, and this a policy decision. The BKs have a £3 million International Centre in London, headquarters at Mount Abu, Rajasthan, India, and several thousand centres world-wide, including Russia and most eastern European countries.

Then there are the organisations based on Buddhist teachings, which are also attracting an increasing number of Western adherents. For many centuries Buddhism, like Hinduism, was hidden in the West, and few people could gain access to any information about it. In the case of Buddhism, the main breakthrough came with the publication in 1975 of a popular book, *Buddhism*, by Christmas Humphreys, a British judge who had been a practising Buddhist for very many years.

Now, there are very many retreats and organisations in the West, each with their devoted followers. The Buddhist movements appeal perhaps to a slightly different type of person than the Hindu movements in that they are quieter, and more intellectual. Many people find Buddhism hard to understand, as the concepts seem to disappear as soon as you imagine you've got hold of them. But, certain types of Buddhism, especially Zen, have always been intimately connected with the human potential

111

movement, and the doctrines intertwine well with the personal growth concepts of self-responsibility, detachment and autonomy.

Lastly, there are one or two other movements which, although they originated in the West, owe a lot to Eastern concepts, such as the Theosophical Society and Science of Mind.

There are, of course, also a number of spurious 'religions' around, such as the Moonies, and Dianetics, or Scientology. Since these movements adopt hard-sell techniques I will leave them severely alone, as most people do not want to be sold religion and, in any case, such an approach goes against the whole ethos of personal growth, which is that you should find your path for yourself, not be dragooned into it.

Neither do I believe that the Mormons, Seventh-Day Adventists or Jehovah's Witnesses, for example, can lead to the kind of personal growth this book is about. So I shan't be including these, either.

These are the main spiritual organisations to have become popular in the West. The list is not exhaustive but, as with the other sections of this book, it describes the kind of thing you can expect if you are attracted to exploring a spiritual path.

HINDU-BASED MODERN SPIRITUAL MOVEMENTS

Until the end of the 1960s, very few people indeed in the West had any knowledge or information on the doctrines of reincarnation and karma, or were aware of the ideas of detachment and surrender. The Eastern spiritual movements, based on ancient Hinduism, were instrumental in bringing these ideas to a mass audience, and they fitted in perfectly with the modern concepts of personal growth.

Because, whether or not one can accept the notion that we possess souls, or spirits, which may be reborn into successive bodies, just taking the possibility on board that physical death is not the end can mean that we will become more responsible and conscious in our actions, and less likely to want to do harm to others. If we become aware that all of our actions rebound on us in some way, we will become far more careful about our actions.

These doctrines, even the most sceptical and cynical among us must agree, make *logical* sense, even if they cannot be proved and even if there is no overwhelming scientific evidence for them. They make harmonious sense – and the whole purpose of personal growth is to establish harmony and beneficial order in the world.

And the concept of detachment, which is that in order to love oneself and others properly, it is essential to detach and see others as separate entities rather than extensions of ourselves, can only be a healthy attitude when confronting addictions, codependency, enmeshed family relations, and all the other dysfunctions which characterise so many modern human relationships.

Detached, unconditional love is the only healthy way to relate to other people, and yet it was virtually an unknown concept until Eastern religions began to be accessible in the West. The Hindu-based movements also taught us that we should strive to see the best in others, rather than run them down, and focus on their good qualities rather than their drawbacks. In this way, we will not accumulate negativity ourselves, and we need no longer see others in a limited, fearful way.

Hindu movements teach that we basically *are* souls – we do not possess them, we are our souls. We are souls who possess bodies, rather than the other way around. When we can see ourselves and other people basically as souls rather than bodies, we will cease to see them as black, white, male, female, children, handicapped, old, young. A child will become a soul in a small body; an old person, a soul in an elderly body. The soul itself is ageless, genderless and has no dimensions. It is merely housed in a highly temporary, physical body.

While the body dies, the soul goes on for ever. Some Hindu organisations believe that human souls always inhabit human bodies, while others teach that, depending on our karma, we may descend to animal or even plant habitations in a future life, or that we have risen from an animal incarnation to our present human form.

Some people can accept these ideas, while for others they will remain nonsensical. The best way to approach modern spiritual movements is to test them and see whether they strike a chord with you, whether they leave you cold or seem to speak directly to you. For some people, the doctrines make intellectual sense, while for others, they make some kind of deep emotional impact.

All the movements described in this chapter are 'genuine' in that they do not ask you to commit huge sums of money, to give up everything to serve the guru, or to go out and convert others. Very many thousands of Westerners have already found them a lifeline, and their influence is becoming more widespread all the time.

The organisations examined below will appeal to people who want a complete experience, emotional, aesthetic and intellectual, as well as practical information on personal growth and transformation. The very exoticness of some of these organisations, with their early morning rising, their ashrams (religious places of retreat) in remote and beautiful parts of India, their gurus and enlightened masters, can all combine to set aspirants on a dedicated path towards true awareness.

Although some Eastern movements have been derided as cults, and seen as encouraging dependent, junkie behaviour, there is no doubt that some have played their part in helping us to see ourselves, other people and what is happening in the world, in a new and more helpful light.

The Brahma Kumaris World Spiritual University

This was founded in India in the 1930s, by a millionaire Sindi jeweller known as Dada Lekraj, who started having visions about the end of the world. From the start, many young women flocked to him and wanted to follow him – young men as well. But the women who tried to join him fared worst, as they were literally locked up and beaten by their families for disobedience and not succumbing to arranged marriages and passive lifestyles.

However, they somehow broke free, continued to flock round Dada, and the movement was gradually established. The University, now with headquarters in Mount Abu, India, is currently dedicating itself as a world-wide organisation for promoting peace. It is affiliated to the United Nations, and regularly holds seminars, conferences and workshops for world leaders at its Rajasthan headquarters.

From the start, Dada Lekraj, who became known as Brahma Baba, promoted women in the movement. There were several reasons for this: one was to redress the balance of centuries; and the other was because, on the whole, women do not have the ego and arrogance of men. It was the first time in India that women had been put forward as spiritual leaders, or given any power of their own.

The Brahma Kumaris are a very ascetic organisation. They recommend total celibacy, both in and out of marriage, believing that sex is a prime source of many ills, both personal and global. It is mainly because of our out-of-control sex lust these days, they believe, that we have an ever-expanding world population. But also, they say, physical sex is anathema to spirituality – the very opposite of the views originally held by Bhagwan Shree Rajneesh, (see above) who preached that through sex it was possible to transcend ordinary consciousness and arrive at a feeling of oneness with the universe.

The BKs also believe that through sex, women have lost their original power and autonomy, and they can reclaim it only when their bodies are not being regularly invaded. The movement is strictly vegetarian and teetotal, although unlike some Hindu-based movements, they do allow tea and coffee.

Members and students try to rise at 4 a.m., and spend an hour in silent meditation. There is always a class at 6.30 a.m., in every centre in the world, where a reading and talk is followed by meditation. Although there is a small core of full-time members, most students are encouraged to continue with their ordinary jobs and live as normal a life as possible.

BKs believe that time is circular, that most of us have had many human incarnations in the past, but that there are always new souls coming down – hence the inexorable rise in the population, despite effective birth control. When all the souls in existence have arrived on earth, the world will end in its present form, and start again with the age of gold. This cycle, they say, has gone on for ever and ever, and will continue to do so. Thus, there is no beginning or end of time.

Although ancient Hindu beliefs form the basis for the movement, the BKs are now specialising in running stress management and positive thinking courses. Empowerment of the individual, and freedom from negative thoughts and habits which are preventing the flowering of true potential, is very much at the forefront of their teaching.

Central is the idea that there can never be world peace until each one of us is peaceful within ourselves. We must work at ourselves first, and become powerful and positive, serene and cheerful, before we can hope to do any good in the world. One of the University's main messages is: world change through individual change.

No charges are ever made for BK courses or conferences, and the centres are financed through donations from members and students. No fundraising activities are ever carried out.

Although initially seen as highly peculiar when it first arrived in the West in the late 1960s – Brahma Baba himself died in 1968 – the

Spiritual University is now able to attract world heads of state and political leaders to its peace initiatives and conferences. It is highly active in India, where it has been campaigning for many years against the dowry system, and for equal education and opportunities for women.

Information on courses and events from: Brahma Kumaris World Spiritual University, Global Co-operation House, 65 Pound Lane, London NW10 2HH. Tel: 081–459 1400.

International Society for Krishna Consciousness

Krishnas are the people who march along high streets in orange robes and with a little tuft of hair allowed to grow long on an otherwise shaved head (men at least). But there is more to them than chanting and banging tambourines.

One of the more 'showbizzy' Eastern movements – several Hollywood stars have been attracted by it, for example Hayley Mills – the International Society, which was actually founded in America, bases its teachings on the *Bhagavad-Gita*, the best-loved of all Hindu scriptures. The movement encourages members to be continent sexually, to be vegetarian and to abstain from alcohol.

The International Society run popular vegetarian restaurants in many capital cities, and interested people can go for a free meal at one of their centres or temples. They also have a catering service, which is extremely popular for functions.

Communion with the Supreme Spirit is seen as the whole point of yoga, and the Society condemns what it sees as the 'commercialisation' of yoga in the form of keep-fit.

Information from: International Society for Krishna Consciousness, Bhaktivedanta Manor, Letchmore Heath, Watford, Herts WD2 8EP. Tel: 0923 857244.

Osho (formerly Bhagwan Shree Rajneesh Organisation)

Just before he died of a heart attack in 1990, Bhagwan Shree Rajneesh changed his name to Osho, Japanese for friend, thus disposing of the Hindu title by which he called himself God.

After its disastrous experiment with an alternative community in Oregon, USA, where it came to resemble a police state, the Rajneeshees regrouped themselves in Poona, India, where their headquarters remain. It is difficult to know now exactly what they are about as, since the death of their leader, the group has undergone many changes.

There is no doubt that Rajneesh was a very remarkable man. A former lecturer in philosophy, he set himself up as a religious leader in Bombay in the late 1960s, when students began to flock round him to hear what he had to say. In the early days, they were all Indian students but, gradually, he began to attract Westerners as well.

His message was certainly revolutionary for the young Indians of the time, as he was telling them to go out and enjoy sex with as many partners as possible. He also preached that true spirituality could come through the orgasm, and thus echoed Wilhelm Reich's work. In fact, Rajneesh was very well read in the Californian human potential movement, and felt that ancient spirituality and modern psychology could come together in a world-wide movement of sexual freedom, peace, love and enlightenment such as the world had never seen before.

Rajneesh, born into a poor family, was a tremendously erudite and learned man who could speed-read up to fifteen books a day. He was a highly charismatic and beguiling speaker, with huge liquid eyes that held his followers spellbound.

The ashrams and groups he set up in India combined dynamic, cathartic meditation with intense sexual experiences based on tantra, where the orgasm was held off for an hour or more, to 'spiritualise' the experience and make it capable of altering consciousness. Although there was an enormous amount of sex taking place at the most famous ashram, in Poona, no children were ever born to Rajneesh's followers. This is because he believed that 90 per cent of people were completely unfit to be parents, and also that most women were burdened, not fulfilled, by pregnancy.

His followers, at least, could liberate themselves from the demands of child-rearing, and do their bit to control the population explosion, by never reproducing. He insisted on sterilisation for both men and women, and any woman who did become pregnant had to have an abortion or leave the community.

In the early days, Rajneesh definitely displayed unusual and compelling powers. But as time went on the organisation became corrupted, Rajneesh's collecting mania led to him amassing nearly a hundred Rolls-Royces, and he himself was addicted to psychotropic drugs. His followers became involved in many illegal activities, and several were given prison sentences, including Rajneesh himself. On his release from prison, no country in the world would have him and he flew from one land to another, eventually apparently disappearing.

His end is shrouded in mystery, and some former followers believe that, during a year or two in America where he went into complete silence, his brother took his place. But loyal followers are still continuing the organisation which, during the 1970s and 1980s, became one of the most talked-about movements in the world, attracting many eminent writers, musicians and actors to the ashrams. The British actor Terence Stamp was given VIP treatment in Poona, and American singer Diana Ross also spent time there.

If nothing else, the amazing, although short-lived, success of the Rajneesh movement indicated just how hungry so many people are for spiritual messages, and how easy it is for highly intelligent, educated people to become influenced by a charismatic, confident man who seems to have a brand-new and timely message for the world.

Just before he died, Rajneesh predicted that three-quarters of the world's population would eventually die of AIDS – and the free-for-all sex was severely curtailed in his ashrams and communities.

Information on retreats and ashrams from: Neo-Sannyas International, Rennweg 34, Ch-8001 Zurich, Switzerland.

Sri Aurobindo

Another Indian guru who became extremely popular in the West, Sri Aurobindo Ghose was born in 1872 and studied at Cambridge. On his return to India, he became a political activist, and was imprisoned. In prison he had a profound mystical experience which led him to study ancient yoga and develop a more modern system which he felt was relevant to the world today.

On his death in 1950, his place was taken by 'The Mother', a Frenchwoman who died in 1974. His ashram, Auroville, at Pondicherry, has become extremely popular with Westerners and was founded as an example of harmonious living.

Information from: Sri Aurobindo Ashram, Auroville, Pondicherry, India.

Sai Baba

The orginal Sai Baba died in 1918, but the one who has become so famous in the West is Sri Satya Sai Baba, who claims to be a reincarnation of the original. Many thousands of Westerners have flocked to his ashram, where he has apparently performed miracles by producing precious jewels out of thin air. The writer Phyllis Krystal, author of the popular *Cutting the Ties that Bind* (Element) – a manual for freeing oneself from outdated attachments and beliefs – is a disciple of Sai Baba. But it is because of his apparent magical abilities that he has become famous in the West and, unlike many modern Indian gurus, Sri Satya Sai Baba has never travelled to the West.

Information from: Sai Baba Ashram, Puttaparti, Andhra Pradesh, Southern India.

Siddha Yoga

The practice of Siddha yoga – the ancient Siddhis were enlightened masters who possessed supernatural powers – was brought over to the West in 1969 by Swami Muktananda. Although full-time adherents are celibate, vegetarian, teetotal and rise at dawn to spend an hour in silent meditation, many people who have become interested in Siddha yoga practise it on a much lighter basis, meditating for half an hour or so a day, but without taking on board the more ascetic aspects.

Siddha yoga is in many ways traditional Hinduism, and teaches reincarnation and the transmigration of souls – that is, we may come back as an animal, insect or plant. Swami Muktananda is dead now, and his place has been taken by a beautiful young Indian woman, Swami Chidvilisa-nanda, whom he appointed as his successor shortly before his death.

Chanting and meditation 'intensives' – which are quite expensive – play a large part in Siddha yoga. During meditation, people often start hyperventilating, groaning and sighing, which can be offputting for the beginner. It is noticeable that men always make more noise than women! Like TM, Siddha yoga has been intensely promoted as a way of reducing stress and helping people to become more effective generally. Many doctors, nurses and other health professionals have attested to its benefits.

Some critics have derided Siddha yoga as 'Hollywood yoga', both because it has attracted many film stars and celebrities, such as Olivia Hussey, and because it can provide a little extra spiritual *frisson* to life without disrupting the status quo too much.

Information from: Siddha Yoga Dham UK, Conford Park House, Conford, Hampshire GU30 7QP. Tel: 0428 725130.

Sivananda Yoga Vedanta Centre

Founded in the nineteenth century by Swami Sivananda, an Indian doctor, this organisation is now world-wide and has a number of centres in Britain, America, Canada and India. Much of the emphasis of Sivananda rests on the five principles of healthy living – proper exercise, proper breathing, proper relaxation, positive thinking and meditation, and a proper diet.

This organisation holds regular hatha yoga classes, which are highly popular. The classes, run by experienced and qualified teachers, have introduced many Westerners to the benefits of yoga breathing and postures – pranayama and asanas. There are also regular meditation intensives, retreats, teachers' training courses, fasting weekends and cooking lessons, both on a day and on a residential basis. In fact, full programmes of events, including concerts, feasts and all-night meditations, are always being held at the centres.

Sivananda yoga comes nearest in its teachings to the Brahma Kumaris World Spiritual University, except that it is less outward-directed in its quest for world peace. The diet is pure vegetarian, and no stimulants of any kind, including tea and coffee, are allowed. Full-time swamis, who have taken vows of celibacy and surrender, wear orange and spend much time in meditation and chanting.

Sivananda yoga is for serious aspirants, it is intensely spiritual, and, like other Eastern movements, is aimed at cultivating the very best human qualities of cheerfulness, positivity and optimism. One of their mottos is: it is your duty to be cheerful.

Income is derived from the yoga courses, conferences and other events. The organisation is a non-profit making charity and charges are kept as low as possible. All full-time workers and teachers are voluntary, and nobody is paid a salary of any kind. There are no vast riches, no Rolls-Royces or luxurious living, although all of the centres have their own special, peaceful atmosphere.

Information from: Sivananda Yoga Vedanta Centre, 51 Felsham Road, London SW15 1AZ. Tel: 081–780 0160. Fax: 081–780 0128.

Transcendental Meditation

This form of meditation, brought to the West by Maharishi Mahesh Yogi, was the first to be specially adapted for Westerners who, having thrown off the shackles of conventional religion, were looking for something which might give meaning and direction to their lives. TM was ideal, as it was spiritual and exotic without being *too* impossibly alien.

From the first, TM was presented as a practical method of reducing stress, and becoming more effective both personally and in the world at large. Members were given a mantra and asked to meditate on this for twenty minutes twice a day – quite a long time, if you've ever tried to do it.

For most people, this is enough. But there are more advanced courses on offer which purport to teach the art of 'yogic flying'. In fact, this has nothing to do with levitation, and is a kind of hopping which can be achieved by anybody who has mastered the lotus position – it is no more 'spiritual' than any other yoga posture, although it takes quite a lot of practice and suppleness to achieve.

Many of the 'real' Eastern movements see TM as spurious, etiolated spirituality. However, it has become the most outstandingly successful meditation movement in the West, and is now highly rich and influential.

It was the first meditation movement to instigate scientific studies into the value of meditation, something which has now been shown in numerous clinical trials to be of great benefit to all body systems.

TM has always denied that it is a religion, although there is a more esoteric side to it than is on offer to the general public, available only for the devotees or members of the inner circle. It does not ask adherents to give up anything such as cigarettes, wine, sex or going to the cinema, unlike both the Brahma Kumaris and the Sivananda Yoga Centres, who recommend no reading of novels, or going to see plays or films, as these disturb mental equilibrium, they believe.

In many ways, TM is the most 'secular' of all the Eastern-based spiritual movements to have become popular over the past twenty years or so, and possibly for this reason it has attracted many thousands of followers. It is heavily into promoting itself and its courses are very expensive. It has tended to attract mainly professional people – doctors, scientists, lawyers, business executives – people whose work tends to be stressful by its very nature.

Unlike many other spiritual movements, TM has never been seen as 'weird' and nobody has ever been ashamed to admit that they practise it. TM has undoubtedly been instrumental in bringing the benefits of meditation to the attention of the medical profession and it is now widely recommended as a way of reducing stress.

Information from: Transcendental Meditation National Office, Mentmore Towers, Leighton Buzzard LU7 0QH.

The School of Meditation

The form of meditation taught in this school is similar to TM in that it is based on meditating on a mantra. Established since 1961, the School teaches students individually, and holds regular discussion groups about the meaning and benefits of meditation.

Information from: School of Meditation, 158 Holland Park Avenue, London W11 4UH. Tel: 071–603 6116.

BUDDHIST ORGANISATIONS

In spite of the influence of Zen Buddhism on the West in the 1950s and 1960s, Buddhist organisations have never made quite the same impact on Westerners as the Hindu-based movements. One reason for this might be that Buddhism is more difficult to understand. Another may be that Buddhism, on the whole, has not attracted the kind of charismatic gurus who have commanded such media attention as Bhagwan Shree Rajneesh, Sai Baba and Maharishi Mahesh Yogi.

A third reason is perhaps that most Buddhist organisations have not been so commercial, so thrusting, as the Hindu-based movements. Even so, Buddhist-derived doctrines have a great appeal to Westerners who dislike the idea of a God, or Supreme Spirit, as in the Hindu religion, and their influence is steadily growing.

Perhaps the best-known Buddhist organisations in the West are those which organise regular retreats, places where the weary, jaded Westerner can find harmony and peace in a spiritual setting.

Buddhism is an extremely intellectual religion that is difficult to grasp, and because of its lack of a central God, it has been called a philosophy rather than a religion. Most people have heard of the Noble Eightfold Path, or Middle Way, which is supposed to steer a sensible course between the extremes of asceticism as practised by some yogis, and pure pleasure-seeking for its own sake. The Path consists of: Right Views, Right Intent, Right Speech, Right Livelihood, Right Action, Right Effort, Right Mindfulness and Right Concentration.

At the heart of the Buddhist doctrine is the idea that all of material life is an illusion, and that the basis of human suffering is desire. Only when we no longer have desires can we be happy. The Noble Eightfold Path is supposed to lead to a cessation of all desires – something most Westerners find peculiar, especially in the days when sexual desire, particularly, is promoted as a goal to aim at, and lack of desire is considered to be some kind of dysfunction.

Buddhists, like Hindus, believe implicitly in karma and reincarnation. The idea is to escape from this incessant wheel of birth and rebirth to attain Nirvana, or the state of nothingness. When all karma has been completed, according to Buddhism, there are no more earthly incarnations.

Through concentration and practice, adepts are supposed to be able to attain magic powers, such as levitation, telepathy, the ability to recall past lives and clairvoyance.

There have been many accounts of Tibetan yogis who can sit out in snow and ice, and melt it by directing heat into various parts of their bodies. Clinical tests on such yogis have shown that they can voluntarily raise their body temperature by about 15°F. But such control takes years and years of practice, and is not the aim of most Westerners studying Buddhism which is, as with any path of personal growth, to attain inner peace and serenity.

Nichiren Soshu

This is the 'modern' type of Buddhism, originating in Japan, and has an enormous following in the West. It is a kind of 'Hollywood Buddhism', and many stars and celebrities follow its precepts. Nichirenism, named after a thirteenth-century saint, became popular during the 1950s in the West and is growing rapidly today, possibly because its places great emphasis on wordly and monetary success, which is certainly not part of the aim of traditional Buddhism.

Members of this organisation, which is particularly popular in America, chant mystical words in order to gain what they wish from life. The idea is that chanting for several hours a day brings about an alteration in consciousness, which can usher in a different, and more positive, reality. Some critics say that Nichiren Soshu is a materialistic cult. It certainly seems to appeal to most to professional people, those who perhaps like the idea of adherence to an exotic Eastern religion, but without having to change their lifestyle in any appreciable way.

Information from: 1 The Green, Richmond, Surrey TW9 1PL. Tel: 081–948 0381/2.

(*Note*: Groups which place a lot of emphasis on chanting in their practices have become especially popular in the West, possibly because nowadays most of us have little chance ever to sing, and because many of us are nervous singing in public anyway. It is significant that several key names in the new age movement, such as Jill Purce and Chris James, teach singing as a way of achieving personal transformation for the better. Both Chris and Jill have learned singing and chanting techniques from the East, and believe that liberating the voice can also liberate much pent-up and negative emotion in us.)

Information on singing workshops: Arnica House, 170 Campden Hill Road, London W8 7AS. Tel: 071–938 3788.

Information on Jill Purce, Mongolian and Tibetan overtone chanting, mantra and sonic meditation available from: Inner Sound and Voice. Tel: 071–607 5819.

Tibetan Buddhism

Tibetan Buddhism has a powerful and increasing hold on many Westerners, some of whom have come to see this form of Buddhism as the purest, and closest to the Buddha's teachings. There are a number of retreats in the West which practise Tibetan Buddhism, and which offer peace and solace to the weary Westerner.

Tibetan Buddhism places emphasis on the unity and connectedness of all life, which is of course one of the cornerstones of the personal growth movement.

The Samyeling Tibetan Centre gives instruction in the elements of Tibetan Buddhism, and also many complementary medical therapies, such as acupuncture, osteopathy and cranio-sacral therapy. This centre is ideal for people who are interested in learning what this form of Buddhism is all about, as there are many classes and workshops for beginners. It is a residential centre, and has been featured in a number of television programmes and newspaper articles.

Information from: Samyeling Tibetan Centre, Eskdalemuir, Langholm DG13 0QL. Tel: 03873 73232.

Also: RIGPA Fellowship, 330 Caledonian Road, London N1 1BB. Tel: 071–700 0185. This Fellowship holds numerous courses in Buddhism of all kinds and specialises in teaching positive attitudes towards death. It concentrates on forming a link between ancient Buddhism and modern psychology, and teaches positive health through mantra chanting, creative visualisation and psychotherapy.

Zen Buddhism

This form of Buddhism, which came to the West from China, has become extremely popular in the West, and books with such titles as *Zen and the Art of Motorcycle Maintenance* and *Zen and the Art of Archery* have become quirky bestsellers. Among the first Westerners to take to Zen philosophy were the Beat Generation of Jack Kerouac, Neal and Carolyn Cassady, and the poet Alan Ginsburg.

Zen students are usually under the guidance of a Zen Master, of whom there are now many in the West. Many people consider Zen to be the most accessible form of Buddhism for Westerners.

Zen Master Hogen, a Japanese, has become one of the most influential Zen teachers in the West. The essence of the philosophy he teaches is as follows. 'Whatever you are doing now, this is your daily reality, and you should not try to escape it. You should place your awareness on the Here and Now, not at some indefinable time in the future.'

Zen Master Hogen teaches that we should not cut ourselves off from material possessions and physical pleasure. There is not necessarily anything to be gained from mindless asceticism.

He says, in common with other Eastern enlightened masters, that the root of all suffering is attachment to the ego, which is a kind of false pride. We should not expect that our lives will be all peace and happiness, but should welcome suffering, as this often acts as a catalyst for personal transformation. All suffering contains important lessons to be learned, and we should always ask ourselves what these lessons are. When we can accept suffering, it disappears. Pain is refusal to accept our present reality, whatever that might be.

All wars, disharmony and negative thinking in the world, according to Hogen, come about because of our closed minds and unwillingness to accept change. We should always be prepared to 'go with the flow', to use the New Age cliché.

If we wish to help other people, we must be free from emotional attachments to them. It is this attachment which causes distress and misery, and ensures that we will never genuinely be able to help them. Compassion can only arise when we are free from emotional entanglements, because it is only then that we can start to see clearly. It is impossible to be both compassionate and have personal desires, as these drive away compassion and make us self-seeking and self-centred, which is anathema to all Buddhist teachings.

Information from: London Zen Society, 19 Belmont Street, London NW1 8HH. Tel: 071–485 9576.

Other Buddhist Centres

The London Buddhist Centre, 51 Roman Road, London E2 0HU. Tel: 081–981 1225.

The Buddhist Society, 58 Eccleston Square, London SW1V 1PH. Tel: 071–834 5858 can provide information on all Buddhist societies, retreats and publications in the UK.

WESTERN SPIRITUAL MOVEMENTS

Science of Mind

This Western spiritual movement, which was founded in America in the 1930s by Dr Ernest Holmes, and which is also known as Religious Science, is very 'New Age' in its outlook, as it places primary emphasis on personal growth and the cultivation of a positive outlook on life. It differs from many Western movements in that it wholeheartedly embraces money, or prosperity, as a force for good. The American writer and counsellor Louise Hay, author of such popular successes as *You Can Heal Your Life*, is a member of the Science of Mind Church.

At the heart of Science of Mind is the idea that we can direct our thoughts, and actually choose what we want to think. Through deliberately cultivating the art of positive thinking, said Ernest Holmes, we can inculcate God-like qualities in ourselves. There are four basic tenets to the philosophy.

1 Everything is mind, and you are part of it.
2 Mind responds and produces according to your believing thought. In other words, you create your own reality.
3 You have the right and power to think what you want to think, therefore you may create desired good conditions for yourself and others.
4 You control your own good, and you may transform your life into an experience of happiness, health and prosperity.

Health, according to Science of Mind adherents, comes about through right thinking. Most illnesses are caused by negative habits of thought, and they can be healed by substituting positive thoughts instead. Bodily conditions are governed by thought processes, and the mind will accept any thought pattern we consistently give it.

According to Science of Mind, nobody need be poor. There is plenty of money in the universe, and we can claim it by having the right kind of thoughts. Your financial success already exists, Ernest Holmes taught – it is just waiting for you to see it and accept it as your own. In order to do this, you have to believe that it is possible, and train yourself to think that it is only natural and right that it should come to you.

Ernest Holmes was not suggesting that people should get money dishonestly, but that by having prosperity consciousness, rather than poverty consciousness, we can already see ourselves as rich, so the money will naturally follow, in much the same way that if we see ourselves as naturally healthy, good health will follow. You must believe in your financial welfare and act as though it is already yours.

But, you must do something to create wealth – offer a service or express yourself in some creative way. One way to feel rich is to have a consciousness of abundance, to pay all your bills gladly and never hand over anything grudgingly. Bless your money as you hand it over, and remind yourself that you are having something in exchange that you would rather have than the money.

When considering spending money, always ask yourself: will this object be of value to me and, because of it, will I be of greater help, inspiration, encouragement or practical help to others? If the answer is yes to these questions, then you can be sure it is right to spend the money.

If you want success, you must ask yourself the following. What, if anything, have I done to deserve it? Have I put my very best efforts into my work? Have I made myself especially proficient in one area? What have I done to earn my desired success?

Above all, you have to regard yourself as an outlet through which health, wealth and success can flow. If everybody made use of their positive qualities, then there would be no lack of harmony, no sadness, ignorance, illness or fear in the world. Science of Mind reminds us that we already have all the good qualities we need, and it's just a matter of recognising them and putting them into action.

In order to eliminate what you don't want, pay no attention to it, and redirect your efforts instead to the exact opposite, to what you really do want. If you feel jealous or envious, try to forget all those mean feelings and let your mind be at peace.

One of the best habits to inculcate is that of cheerfulness – a message that runs through all the personal growth organisations and movements encountered so far. Over the years, most of us have built up negative tendencies and habits, and it will take time to strip these away from the consciousness. Always plant good seeds in the mind, remembering that the bad seeds will grow as quickly as the nourishing plants, possibly even quicker.

Always strive to see the good in other people, and the good in yourself. Never think of yourself as inferior or superior, but be glad of the gifts you have, seeking always to enlarge them and put them in the service of humanity. When you express approval of a person, says Holmes, you set a standard they will then try to keep up. If you express disapproval, the opposite happens, and people may become crushed and despondent. Never be the cause of this in others.

Science of Mind Centres and Churches have become very popular in America and Europe, and attract people who wish to maximise their potential, and remind themselves constantly that thought is the source of all actions – something which the ancient Hindu and Buddhist scriptures all made clear centuries ago, but which we have tended to lose sight of in the twentieth century.

Information from: The Bloomsbury Hall, St Georges Churchyard, Bloomsbury Way, London WC1. Tel: 081–551 8773 or 071–352 4046. Offers regular, free public lectures on Science of Mind philosophy.

Also: Thomas Troward Society, 20 Grove Park, London E11 2DL. Tel: 081–505 9098. Thomas Troward was a lawyer who later embraced Science of Mind. The Society holds counselling sessions to put people in touch with their own latent creative powers.

The New Church

Not all that new now, this movement began in 1788 to further the work of Emmanuel Swedenborg, a Swedish scientist who, in his fifties, suddenly became a mystic and visionary. He believed he was in direct communication with spirits, and also became psychic and clairvoyant.

The New Church is basically Christian, and believes in the wisdom of the Bible and in Jesus Christ as the Son of God. The 'personal growth' aspect of the teachings are that everything which happens to us in this world can be used as a learning experience, and that all sufferings, setbacks and reversals can be used to strengthen character.

The New Church sees the religious writings of Swedenborg as a revelation directly from God, and runs courses, seminars and retreats for those who are interested in studying the Bible and Christianity from a Swedenborg perspective.

An organisation such as the New Church would be suitable for those who do not wish to leave their Christian roots, but who have not found that standard churches are facilitating their own personal growth.

Information from: The Swedenborg Movement, Oaklands New Church Centre, Winleigh Road, Birmingham B20 2HN. Tel: 0959 534220.

Christian Community

This is one of the many projects of Rudolf Steiner, the Austrian teacher and philosopher who turned his attention to medicine, education and agriculture, as well as more innately spiritual matters. This Community was formed in 1922 to bring home the essential message of Christianity, which is not all that different to the Eastern traditions, as it places major emphasis on personal growth. According to Steiner, reincarnation is at the heart of genuine Christianity, and the resurrection and sacraments can be seen as symbols of personal growth.

Information from: Christian Community, Temple Lodge, 51 Queen Caroline Street, London W6 9QL. Tel: 081–748 8388.

Information on other aspects of Steiner's work: The Anthroposophical Association, Rudolf Steiner House, London NW1. Tel: 071–723 4400.

White Eagle Lodge

This was founded in 1936 by Grace Cooke to further the teachings of her spirit guide, White Eagle, and to help people to overcome their fear of death by helping them to see that the spirit is more important than the obviously temporary body. Meetings, seminars, retreats and conferences are held at the Lodge, which is expanding its activities all the time, even though it is now many years since the death of the founder.

Information from: The White Eagle Lodge, 9 St Mary Abbots Place, London W8 6LS. Tel: 071–603 7914.

The Theosophical Society

This Society (founded in 1875) continues the work of Madame Helena Blavatsky, the Russian adventuress and religious prophet, who taught that in essence all religions are preaching the same message, and that we should look for the similarities, rather than the differences. Theosophism was instrumental in introducing the ideas of rebirth and karma to the West, as Madame Blavatsky was supposedly taught her doctrines – enshrined in her book *The Secret Doctrine* – by Buddhist Masters in Tibet. Whether or not she ever went to Tibet is, like much of her life, shrouded in mystery.

One of theosophy's most eminent members, Dr Ian Stevenson, has for several decades been trying to prove reincarnation by scientific methods. He has also introduced the idea to a wider audience and, if he has not managed to prove conclusively that we have lived before, has at least ensured that it is now taken seriously by scientists, churchmen and serious thinkers everywhere.

Information from: The Theosophical Society, 50 Gloucester Place, London W1H 3HJ. Tel: 071–935 9261.

Gurdjieff Ouspensky School

This School teaches that whatever happens to us, and whatever the circumstances we find ourselves in, are exactly right for us at the time, because they are enabling us to learn from them. Gurdjieff and Ouspensky, his main pupil, brought many of their ideas from the East,

131

and codified them into a form which was considered suitable for Westerners. Bhagwan Shree Rajneesh was highly influenced by Gurdjieff, one of whose tenets was that people should be put into difficult circumstances to aid their own personal growth. We should see everything that is happening to us as valuable, and see what we can gain from the experience, rather than trying to deny it. Many Westerners find Gurdjieffian teachings impossibly difficult and harsh, although he is now seen as one of the great spiritual leaders of our time.

Information from: New World, Box 1531, London NW3 6RW. Tel: 081–786 7094.

Beshara Trust

This Trust was set up to provide a centre for people to come and discuss spiritual matters without having to adhere to any particular religious dogma.

Information from: Frilford Grange, Frilford, nr Abingdon, Oxon OX3 5NX. Tel: 0865 391344.

MIDDLE AND NEAR-EASTERN SPIRITUAL MOVEMENTS

Sufism

Sufism is the mystical aspect of Islam, which has inspired much poetry and devotional literature. The *Rubáiyát of Omar Khayyám* is one of the best-known Sufi works. The actual word Sufi derives from the simple woollen garments worn by early Muslim devotees in the desert, when they were engaged on a meditative and inward search. Whirling dervishes are Sufis, people who danced until they collapsed in ecstasy.

Sufism also places emphasis on the value of erotic love, of dance and ecstatic experiences in general.

Sufism is attracting an ever-growing number of followers in the West because of its mystical tradition. Unlike other branches of Islam, which can seem cold and forbidding to outsiders, with a set of rules to be obeyed whatever, Sufism has poetic, literary and meditative appeal.

You do not have to have a Muslim background to be interested in Sufism. It tends to appeal to romantic-minded people, those who are avid for intense experiences, for feeling, rather than a more intellectual approach to their self-development.

Information from: Four Winds Centre, High Thicket Road, Temple Hill, Dockenfield, Farnham, Surrey GU10 4HB. Tel: 025125 3990.

The Baha'i Faith

Again very popular with Westerners, this faith basically teaches the oneness of all humanity and of all religions. Founded in Persia in the nineteenth century, there are no priests or clergy, but communities who meditate, work and pray together. There is emphasis on hard work and service to humanity. The Baha'i faith is now believed to be the most widely spread religion after Christianity.

Information from: 27 Rutland Gate, London SW7 1PD. Tel: 071– 584 2566.

Retreats

Retreats of all spiritual denominations – and none – are becoming increasingly popular as ever more people are seeking an opportunity to escape from the stress and pollution, both internal and external, of everyday life.

Retreats, which are almost always residential, are usually highly structured, and offer an opportunity for peace and quiet, as well as lectures, workshops or courses. Most retreats are large country houses, often in beautiful grounds, and many offer the chance of an intense spiritual experience.

The best ones, to my mind, combine meditation, lectures or workshops, with discussion and work and exercise programmes, so that each day is filled with a variety of interesting activities. You don't have to be religious, or spiritual, or even looking for some kind of experience, in order to benefit from a retreat. All you need to take with you is an open mind, and a willingness to listen to those who might have a different outlook on life to yours.

There are now very many retreat centres in the UK, and all are slightly different. Retreats can be seen as a holiday with a purpose. Although most are set in beautiful surroundings, they are mainly inexpensive, and accommodation may be somewhat primitive or shared. Don't expect five-star hotel treatment, even in the most beautiful and idyllic surroundings.

Opinions differ on whether it is better to go to a retreat by yourself, or with a friend or partner. My own view is that it's more beneficial to go by yourself, as it can be difficult to attend wholeheartedly to your own personal growth when there is somebody else to consider. Also, never worry about being lonely or isolated on a retreat. There will always be plenty of people to talk to and, as you have a common purpose, you will be almost sure to find kindred spirits. At least all the others on the retreat will be serious thinkers and seekers – otherwise they wouldn't be there.

There is now a Retreat Association, which publishes a magazine called *The Vision*, listing all the main retreats in the country, including one or two in central London.

Write to: The National Retreat Association, 24 South Audley Street, London W1Y 5DL. Tel: 071–493 3534.

(*Note*: Most, if not all, retreats offer vegetarian catering only and there is no alcohol.)

Sivananda Yoga Vedanta Centre

This Centre, described earlier in this section on pages 120–121, organises many retreats in several parts of the world. I attended one in Nassau, Bahamas – which sounds exotic enough.

The day began at 5.30 a.m., when we were awakened by a clanging bell that it was impossible to sleep through. A meditation and chanting session came first, followed by a talk. Then there was a yoga class, lasting one and a half hours. After that came breakfast, then 'karma yoga' – jobs such as cooking, cleaning, addressing envelopes. Around noon there were talks and lectures, then some free time. Another yoga class came at 4 p.m., followed by supper at 6, and the main lecture programme of the day, which took place between around 7 and 10 p.m. The day finished with meditation and chanting, and we went to bed around 11. Accommodation was in simple wooden huts or tents, mainly shared.

The Sivananda Centre runs similar retreats at a number of venues in Scotland, Wales and France, and also holds teacher training courses, intensive month-long retreats where physical and mental yoga are taught on a daily basis. These teacher training courses are extremely popular with people who are serious about developing their yogic abilities, both physical and mental.

Morning Light Holiday Retreat and Healing Centre

This is a rapidly expanding centre near Pitlochry, where people can come just for bed, breakfast and evening meal, to take part in the healing services, or to have intensive psychotherapy. There is no charge made for the counselling and psychotherapy sessions, and you don't have to have them if you don't want to. The Centre is run on broadly Christian principles, and offers aromatherapy, spiritual healing, Alexander Technique and other complementary therapies, as well as psychotherapy. A small charge is made for some of the complementary therapies, just to cover costs, and not to make a profit.

Information from: Dalcroy Farm, Tummel Bridge, nr Pitlochry, Perth, Scotland PH16 5NT. Tel: 08824 230.

Insight

This residential centre is in a lighthouse, situated on ley lines, and near the sea. What more could a New Age seeker want? The bedrooms are wedge-shaped, and the centre offers pyramid healing. Quite a heady experience all round!

Information from: Insight, Lighthouse Road, St Bridges, Wentlooge, nr Newport, Gwent NP1 9SF.

Gaunts House

One of the longest-established retreats, this centre offers a number of specialised courses and workshops, and sleeps over 100 people. Courses on offer include: Alexander Technique, 'Relationships: Do you run them or do they run you?'; 'Cutting the Ties that Bind' with Phyllis Krystal; dance techniques; experience and renewal weeks; spiritual and personal development weeks; singing; contacting the inner child – in fact, all the aspects of personal growth we have been talking about so far.

Gaunts House is set in beautiful countryside in Wimborne, Dorset, and there is also a small retreat house, Ashton Lodge, nearby, which specialises in meditation experience.

Information from: Gaunts House, Wimborne, Dorset BH21 4JQ. Tel: 0202 841522.

The Centre of Light

This is a retreat in the Scottish Highlands designed to help you get back in touch with nature, and connect with your innermost being. The idea is to heal the present by letting go and releasing the hurt of the past. There are healing sessions, individual and group work, and meditation, as well as guided walks by rocks, mountains and waterfalls to restore a sense of harmony.

Details from: Linda Christie, Tighnabruaich, Struy, Beauly, Inverness IV4 7JU. Tel: 046 376 245.

Chapter 6

Healing Treatments

Introduction

It is very often the case that a severe health crisis will serve to catapult people into examining their lives and precipitate them into journeying along a path of personal growth. While it is certainly not the case that suffering is always necessary for growth to occur, the fact is that for very many people, it simply does not occur to them to think seriously about their lives and attitudes, their choices, their relationships or work until a serious crisis happens to them. And for many, there is no more serious crisis than a breakdown in health – especially for those who have previously been healthy.

Health is something most of us take absolutely for granted until some illness strikes, and then there are commonly feelings of resentment, hostility, anger and the questions: Why me? What have I done to deserve this?

When there is illness or disease, it is rarely the case that conventional medical treatments will help towards self-transformation. Orthodox medicine, such as is taught in conventional medical schools, tends to see people as a disparate collection of body parts, and simply concentrates on getting the offending part in working order, much as one might take a car to a garage for repair.

Since the early 1980s though, there has been an increasing emphasis on holistic health, which addresses the whole person, and not just the broken leg or even the diseased liver. The idea of holistic health has now penetrated through to the medical profession, after a long struggle, and more doctors than ever before are trying to see their patients as human beings first and foremost, rather than simply as a broken leg, a headache or an infertility problem.

There is now, even among the most diehard conservative members of the medical profession, an increasing awareness that mental and emotional functioning often play their part in bodily illnesses, and also a growing understanding that 'sickness of the spirit' is just as real as physical illness. Sometimes the manifestation of discord or dysfunction is physical, sometimes mental or emotional; more often it is a combination of both.

Of course, these ideas are not new; they have just been lost sight of in the era of technological medicine, and the heyday of the drugs revolution. We are now learning to our cost that very few pills, if any, are really as magic or curative as they might seem and that, very often, the placebo effect works just as much for pharmaceutical drugs as it does for more gentle methods of healing. When new drugs first come on to the market, they often seem wonderful, genuine advances, or miracle cures. Then, after a few years, they seem less effective until, eventually, they are hardly effective at all.

Not only that, but the adverse side-effects from many strong drugs have meant that, in many cases, people would rather have the illness than continue to take the drug. The more serious the illness, the more likely this is to happen. Some cancer drugs, for instance, have been withdrawn owing to their adverse side-effects.

Family doctors are now placing much less emphasis on prescribing pills to treat emotional or stress-related complaints, but are increasingly using counsellors and spiritual healers as part of their health promotion programmes. Some are even training to be counsellors or healers themselves, and there is growing acceptance of the idea that gentle touch, kind words, empathy and understanding, can often do far more to heal than all the drugs and surgery in the world.

Of course, there are times when we may *need* drugs and surgery – few people, apart from Christian Scientists perhaps, would rule these out altogether. But most of the illnesses which plague us today are not those which respond readily to harsh drug regimes. They are, rather, the chronic complaints, the migraines, stress, feelings of general malaise, a perceived inability to get one's life together, or to build up permanent resistance to allergies, viruses, immune disorders.

Those who have studied self-transformation are aware that illnesses, much like any other crisis in life, can be used to teach us important lessons about ourselves. Any form of health crisis can be seen as a 'transformation waiting to happen', in the words of Marilyn Ferguson, author of *The Aquarian Conspiracy* (J. P. Tarcher). We can, she says, either confront the crisis so that the transformation process may begin, or we can deny it, and simply refuse to accept that, in order to be well, we should take a clear, hard look at our lives so far, and see what we can do to change or improve them. But even if we cannot change our lives very much, we can always improve our attitudes, to ourselves, our illness and those around us.

All too many people feel that they are victims, caught up in circumstances beyond their control, and that illness is something which strikes unfairly out of the blue. In fact, this is hardly ever the case. Some therapists adhere to the view that we choose our own illnesses, in a sense, and that they come about through persistent negative thinking and habits.

It can take tremendous courage to face up to illness, as it may involve looking inwards, thinking about the choices we have made, why we have made them and why they have perhaps made us ill. This is why people often need a serious health breakdown before they are able to reflect on their lives. If nothing else, a health breakdown gives us 'time out' from work and other responsibilities so that there is opportunity to think and plan ahead.

The reward for this close, searching look at our lives is, says Marilyn Ferguson, well worth the initial scariness. There will emerge a new harmony, a new peace, a new direction and a new feeling of being in charge, rather than at the mercy of remorseless events. Even though, in some cases, the illness might not be reversible, it is always possible to cultivate a serene, optimistic attitude, to spread genuine cheerfulness rather than despondency.

One of the most important messages to come out of the self-transformation movement in recent years is that all healing is ultimately self-healing. Although some healers are very gifted indeed, all that even the best can do is to help set the self-healing process in motion. Even the most wonderful healer in the world can do little for the person who does not sincerely want to be well – and there are more of those around than you might imagine.

Healing, like any other aspect of personal growth, can take place only when you personally feel you are ready for it. For some people, a very severe crisis indeed may be needed before they gain the strength, anger or courage to look squarely at their lives.

For Anita, a fall which seriously injured her back and meant that she was out of work for months, was 'the best thing that ever happened to me'. As she says:

'I was up in the attic, clearing some stuff out when I stepped on to some rotten floorboards, and fell down to the room below. I was in terrible pain, and was rushed to hospital. As it happened, I hadn't broken any bones, but I kept having agonising backache long after the accident. I went to doctors, but they could do nothing except give me painkillers.

'Eventually I went to a chiropractor, who started manipulating my back and told me there was an old injury there which I must have had as a small child. As he began to manipulate my back, all I could remember was that at the age of six, my parents had divorced.

'I had repressed this memory, but I had carried the hurt around in my body all my adult life, without every really being aware of it. After sessions with the chiropractor, I started going to consciousness-raising classes, and for group therapy. All this gave me the courage to start looking at my own life, and realising why I had never really fulfilled my potential.

'I realised that I had been full of hurt and resentment, and had never worked through my feelings as an adult, but had tried to anaesthetise them through marriage and children – all the usual routes. Once I learned how much I had been sabotaging myself, always taking jobs that were below my capacity, and never really facing up to what I wanted, I gained the courage to change my life for the better.

'I have now embarked, for the first time in my life, on a fulfilling career, and I can see my life with much greater clarity. And it would never have happened but for that back injury.'

After a severe stroke, Paul feared he might never speak properly again. His left side had become paralysed. He had retired from the Army after many years as a career officer, and had no real idea what to do with himself. But, as he said:

'I was determined not to let the stroke beat me. I had followed a completely conventional career and lifestyle with public school, Oxford, the army, marriage and children, and had never been in the slightest bit interested in spiritual or alternative matters.

'But I felt I had to do something after the stroke, otherwise I was never going to be able to enjoy my retirement. Somebody told me about

the Silva Method [described on pages 72–74] and I went along. That was the start of my transformation.

'By using the method, and being able to get into the alpha state, I was able to cure the paralysis, and walk and talk again. In fact, I became completely cured. I then decided to investigate healing further, and began to realise the major part the mind plays.'

The outcome of Paul's recovery was that he started one of the very first 'alternative' healing approaches for cancer sufferers and, for many years, he held spiritual healing sessions at his house.

These are just two examples of people whose lives were transformed for the better for having to face up to a serious illness. This is not to say that we all have to get ill before we can grow, of course – only that illnesses should not be seen as something entirely negative or undesirable. Sometimes, it can be just what we need to get us out of old, unhelpful mindsets, and into new, more nourishing and life-enhancing attitudes.

The writer and counsellor Louise Hay, whose books on self-transformation have been bestsellers on both sides of the Atlantic, found that her path to self-awareness began when she had vaginal cancer diagnosed, and realised that she did not want to be cut up by doctors. Her feeling was that the cancer had appeared for deep-seated reasons she would do well to look at. She healed herself by deciding she did not want to be cut up, and visualised and imagined herself being well. When she recovered, she decided to dedicate her life to understanding the nature of illness, and helping others who had been in similar situations to herself.

So how do you set about finding the healing treatment that may be best for you? If you have a specific complaint then, of course, it makes sense to try the therapy or treatment which is designed to address that particular problem. For instance, if you are plagued with agonising backache, you may consider osteopathy or chiropratic, both of which have been found to be far more effective than standard doctors' treatments, which could make the condition worse.

If your condition is chronic, if you suffer from persistent migraines, have peculiar phobias or obsessions, or cannot seem to enjoy life or get out of difficult circumstances, then you may like to try one of the more exploratory therapies, which try to get to the very bottom of your complaint.

You will discover that your quest for health inevitably invites you to ask yourself searching questions about your lifestyle, relationships, attitudes – and how these might have contributed to your current health problem. Very often, the mere decision to do something about a condition or emotion that has been troubling you for some time means that the journey has started.

All health problems are a cry from the body, the mind and the spirit, to do something about the situation, not to ignore it. All pain is there for a purpose, to draw attention to something important, not for its perception to be covered up with drugs, painkillers or other anaesthetics. It is only when we can address the root cause of the pain that we can understand why it is there, and what we should best do about it.

Here is a guide to some of the more important and effective complementary therapies which have emerged in the past few years, and which are gradually taking their place alongside the more conventional medical treatments, no longer despised as cranky or discounted as 'fringe'.

Acupuncture

This ancient Chinese method of sticking needles into you has been proven in clinical trials to be effective for many kinds of pain relief. There are about 800 different acupuncture points on the body, but nobody has ever quite been able to get to the bottom of why the system works.

The theory is that there are several 'meridians' or sensitive points on the body and, if these can be activated, they channel energy and speed up the healing process. An acupuncturist will first take a very detailed case history, take several pulse points and then insert the needles. There is usually no pain involved, and the needles only go in a little way. Also, they are extremely fine.

Treatments usually last for about an hour, usually in a course of six sessions, although, of course, the number will depend on the nature of your complaint. Acupuncture and acupressure, where the same points are activated with finger and thumb rather than with needles, are good for chronic pain such as headaches, migraines and hay fever. Acupuncture has also been successfully used as a pain reliever during childbirth.

Information on reputable acupuncturists from: The Institute for Complementary Medicine, PO Box 194, London SE16 1QZ. Tel: 071–273 5165.

Aikido

One of the many Japanese martial arts, the idea behind aikido, which first became popular during the 1950s, is to develop the spirit of co-operation and harmony between people, rather than the kind of conflicts that lead to war.

Very much connected with personal growth, aikido (the word means 'the way to the life force') is concerned with helping people bring all their own energies, physical, mental and emotional, into harmony both with each other and the world around. As with other Eastern martial arts, the object of aikido is not to use your own strength on the opponent, but to use his or her strength in your own self-defence.

'Winning' is not the aim of the game, but rather, to aid development of two bodies and minds in harmony with each other, to discover your own and the other's strengths and weak points. Aikido can be used as a form of self-defence, but is perhaps more useful as a way of developing strength, grace and mental strength. You do not need to be physically strong to become adept at aikido.

The art of aikido is usually taught in classes of about twenty, and a uniform of loose trousers, jacket and belt is worn. Some classes insist on strict discipline, such as absolutely accurate time-keeping and physical cleanliness. As aikido is done without shoes or socks, some teachers will not admit potential pupils with even slightly smelly feet.

Information from: The British Ki Aikido Association, 48 Oakshott Court, Polygon Road, London NW1 1ST. Tel: 071–281 0877.

Also: Martial Arts Commission (information on all martial arts and unarmed combat), 1st Floor, Broadway House, 15–16 Deptford Broadway, London SE8 4PE. Tel: 081–691 3433.

Alexander Technique

This bodywork technique can be an excellent starting point on the road to transformation. People often book up Alexander lessons when then have excruciating backache which won't seem to respond to anything else. But, by going for Alexander lessons, patients – or pupils as they are known in Alexander terminology – can come to realise why they may have developed the back or posture problem in the first place.

Healing Treatments

Alexander teachers believe that back problems do not suddenly develop, but are the result of years of bad usage and incorrect posture, which may itself have developed in response to some deep-seated emotional problem. An Alexander teacher will gradually guide you towards correct posture, help you to unlearn all the bad postural habits you have most probably got into, and explain why all your joints and muscles are now troubling you.

According to F. Matthias Alexander, who developed the technique, we get into bad habits of sitting, standing and walking, when we pay more attention to the end goal than the 'means whereby'. By paying attention to the means, rather than just the end, we can learn how to perform simple, everyday tasks without undue strain and effort, and bring actions which have become unconscious through daily repetition, back into conscious awareness.

Alexander teachers place great emphasis on bodily awareness, which may be the first step on the path towards other kinds of awareness. When paying attention to health, whatever increases awareness in one area will inevitable raise consciousness in another. Going for Alexander lessons is a good way of getting to know yourself, and putting yourself back in touch with your body and how it works.

All too often, we just ignore our bodies until they start to play up – by which time undoing the damage may take a lot of time and effort.

For many people, what is attractive about the Alexander technique is that you don't have to take your clothes off, or learn any special routines. The therapy is usually offered on a one-to-one basis, and the teacher will explain everything you have to do.

A useful Alexander method of relaxation you can do at any time is to lie on the floor, supporting your head with books until your spine is completely flat on the floor. Then bend your knees and keep your arms down by your side. Stay in this position for about fifteen minutes without moving – more difficult than it looks – and you will discover that your body is brought into alignment, and your aches and pains start to go. Breathe deeply as you lie still. This is a good exercise to practise whenever you feel tired and tense.

Information from: Society of Teachers of the Alexander Technique, 10 London House, 266 Fulham Road, London SW10 9EL. Tel: 071–351 0828.

Aromatherapy

Since aromatherapy first become widely available in the mid-1980s, it has been surrounded by controversy. Some scientists and researchers have said that the essential oils used in aromatherapy can cause miscarriages and deformities during pregnancy; other authorities have insisted that aromatherapy is all a hoax and a con, and that the oils do nothing whatever.

It has been established, however, that certain essential oils do have definite pharmacological effects, although whether this happens in the quantities used in ordinary cosmetic-type aromatherapy, it is difficult to say.

But, apart from anything else, it is a highly pleasant sensation to lie on a table and be gently massaged with sweet-smelling oils. And at the very least, such massage helps to put you back in touch with your body, to learn to love yourself a bit more than perhaps you did before.

Even the act of allowing somebody, usually a complete stranger, to massage your body, shows that you are opening up and gaining trust in others. Very many people are afraid of massage, afraid of being in this vulnerable position, even when they know that the masseur is not going to do them any harm.

Expert aromatherapy massage will reveal where there may be stress, undue pressure on joints or muscles, or knotted joints caused by sitting in a cramped position for too long, such as while driving.

My own experience of aromatherapy has been extremely therapeutic. Nobody should ever feel that so-called beauty treatments are trivial, or to be discounted. Whatever helps us to look better on the outside will have its corresponding effect on the mind and attitude – and, at the very least, release us from some small burden of worry and concern.

Aromatherapy is now being used extensively in hospitals for chronic, terminal and elderly patients. And, far from being considered trivial in France, you have to be a qualified doctor to practise aromatherapy.

Information on aromatherapy from: International Federation of Aromatherapists, 4 Eastmearn Road, London SE21 8HA. Send sae with your request. The Institute for Complementary Medicine, address on page 143, can supply details of reputable aromatherapists who will treat medical conditions.

Astrology

Astrology is increasingly being used for healing, for past-life therapy and for character assessment. Although very ancient, the subject is still shrouded in controversy and science has so far failed to prove convincingly that the position of the planets can affect destiny on earth. It seems more than likely that there is 'something' in it, although to what extent character may be influenced by the position of planets at birth has so far eluded researchers.

In the past, astrology was used mainly to foretell events, but now it is being combined with psychology, psychotherapy and counselling. Most therapists and complementary healers use astrology as one of their tools, rather than relying on it absolutely. At the very least, astrology is interesting – and as long as it is used for character interpretation, rather than to foretell the future, it is unlikely to do any harm. It is still used widely in the East to pair up suitable partners for arranged marriages.

For astrological counselling, contact: Astro-psychotherapeutical Practice, 23 Whitehall Gardens, London W3 9RD. Tel: 081–992 9514. **Also**: Soul Directed Astrology. Tel: 081–643 4898.

Autogenic Training

This is a Westernised form of meditation or yoga, whereby apparently involuntary bodily functions can be brought under conscious control. The technique was first developed by Johan Schultz in the 1930s. He was a German neurologist who discovered that warmth and relaxation could be consciously induced – something ancient yogis have always known.

Schultz felt that these ancient techniques could be used for modern twentieth-century illnesses, such as stress and high blood pressure. Patients are taught to give parts of their bodies instructions, such as: my left arm feels heavy and tired. The left arm will then respond to the instruction from the mind. In most cases, autogenic training has to be taught by an expert, after which it can be induced when necessary, such as when feeling under pressure, when trying to cope with traffic, or when in particularly stressful or trying circumstances.

One reason autogenic training should be taught by an expert is that often there can be strong emotional reactions, and it is not unknown for people to break down in tears or to start hyperventilating during a session.

Autogenic training first became popular in the UK in the late 1970s, and is increasingly becoming accepted by the medical profession. Indeed, many doctors are now learning and practising it themselves. It is a good way in to self-transformation for many people, as it enables you to control body states you may have considered to be completely involuntary. In this way, you can gradually come to gain control over other aspects of your behaviour you may have considered involuntary, such as being angry, resentful or guilty.

Autogenic training can be a good way of taking charge of what happens to you, and reducing anxiety and stress-related conditions.

Information from: Centre for Autogenic Training, 101 Harley Street, London W1N 1DF. Tel: 071–935 1811.

Ayurveda

This ancient form of Indian medicine is now becoming popular in the West and is being heavily promoted by the transcendental meditation movement. It is a completely holistic form of medicine which may involve taking herbs, exercise, conventional medicines, special diet, breathing, yoga, urine therapy (yes, drinking it!) and minerals.

As with acupuncture, a detailed case history is taken at the outset, together with thirty-two pulse rates, and a specialised regime is prescribed. In the early 1990s, there were claims that ayurveda could cure AIDS, but these claims have not been substantiated. However, it can be said that this type of medicine can certainly help to strengthen the immune system, and can be recommended as a gentle form of treatment for chronic and serious illnesses.

Details from: Association of Auyrvedic Practitioners, 7 Ravenscroft Avenue, London NW1 0SA. Tel: 081–455 3909.

Biodynamics

This is a hands-on massage treatment developed by Gerda Boyesen, who was a Reichian analyst, as well as being a physiotherapist. She came to the conclusion that repressed emotions, and ancient hurts and wounds often remained trapped in the form of waste fluids between nerves and muscles in the body, and that special massage could disperse this, and clear the system.

With biodynamics, the therapist listens with a stethoscope to the noises being made by the abdomen, as trapped fluids and waste products are being dispersed. The massage is tough rather than gentle, and is often of great help with digestive problems, as well as stress, anxiety and repressed emotions.

Information: Biodynamic massage is available at many holistic centres throughout the UK. Trained therapists can be contacted through Gerda Boyesen Centre for Biodynamic Psychology and Psychotherapy, Acacia House, London W3 7JX. Tel: 081–743 2437.

Bioenergetics

This is similar to biodynamics in that it is a form of body-oriented psychotherapy which stems from Reich's theories about repressed emotions being held in body systems. Bioenergetic psychotherapists treat the body and mind as one, and acknowledge that our passage through life is at least partly governed by our physical attributes. The world looks different to a lean, elegant six-footer than to a stocky, dumpy person of five-foot four. In many far-reaching ways, body differences affect our personality and outlook.

Bioenergetic exercises include deep breathing, making faces, coughing, yawning, kicking, pounding, stamping – whatever you need to do to release your pent-up emotions and 'body armour'.

Very often, working on the body in this way activates old, painful memories and brings them to the surface. It is a kind of 'clearing' therapy, and the idea is that it helps you to become friends with your body, to realise that you are living in a body – something many people in the late twentieth century are in danger of forgetting, as we use our bodies less and less in our daily work.

Details about qualified practitioners from: Institute of Bioenergetic Medicine, 103 North Road, Parkstone, Poole, Dorset BH14 0LU. Tel: 0202 733762.

Biofeedback

This technique is now extremely well-established as a reliable method of stress control. Like autogenic training, it is a method of bringing the functions of the autonomic nervous system under conscious control, and uses electronic equipment to monitor heart and pulse rate, skin resistance and slight increases in temperature. Biofeedback machines are now used in many hospitals and doctors' surgeries in order to enable stressed patients to monitor their own level of relaxation.

Biofeedback machines enable people to discover for themselves what goes on in meditation: the deeper the meditation, the slower and more regular the brainwaves are. Simple relaxation meters cost around £100.

Information about biofeedback from: Centre for Stress Management, 156 Westcombe Hill, London SE3 7DH. Tel: 081–293 4114.

The Bristol Cancer Help Centre

Since it was opened by Prince Charles in 1983, this Centre, which concentrates on alternative healing therapies for people who have already had cancer diagnosed, has become world-famous. But, in 1990, reports that patients who attended Bristol fared worse than those who only had conventional cancer treatment rocked the alternative and complementary medicine world to its foundations.

Later research showed that the whole project had been flawed, as the women who fared worse at the Bristol Centre were far more ill than the controls; in other words, they were not comparing like with like. But the damage had been done, and Bristol has had to rebuild its reputation almost from scratch.

The Bristol Centre pioneered the idea that we should take responsibility for our own illness, and not just rely on the drugs and surgery offered by doctors and hospitals. People who went to Bristol learned as much about themselves as their cancer: through diet, guided visualisation, relaxation therapy and group therapy they were able to take stock of their lives, gain insights as to why and how their cancer might have taken hold, and become more confident and assertive in their handling of the disease.

Very many Bristol patients recovered completely, although no claims were ever made for a cure. One of the cornerstones of its 'gentle' treatment was a non-toxic diet, considered extremely cranky at first, but now taken seriously by cancer experts. The Bristol approach has revolutionised the whole treatment of cancer, and the way patients are now regarded. It has led to a nationwide network of cancer self-help groups and support groups being set up, and a new way of looking at the disease.

The positive approach has meant that many cancer survivors are able to see their illness as the best thing that happened to them, as it enables them to look closely at their lives and make dramatic changes for the better.

Information from: The Bristol Cancer Help Centre. Tel: 0272 7413216.

Colonic Irrigation

Here, the insides are washed out and detoxified with gentle water pressure. It is like a big-time enema, and can be useful for sufferers of candida albicans, ME or chronic fatigue syndrome, and digestive problems. People who have had it say it is not painful, and the sensation of having warm water swishing around your intestines is actually quite pleasant.

Still very controversial, it is gradually gaining ground as colon health is increasingly being seen as a key to a general bodily health. Wastes build up easily in the colon and can be difficult to disperse.

Details about colon irrigation, also known as colon hydrotherapy: International Colon Hydrotherapy Foundation, 27 Warwick Avenue, London W9 2PS. Tel: 071–289 7000. **Also**: The Hale Clinic, 7 Park Crescent, London NW1N 3HE. Tel: 071–631 0156.

Colour Therapy

There are several types of colour therapy. One very ancient therapy consists of clearing and cleaning the aura around people. According to some healers, we all have an aura around us, and this can look clear and bright, or grey and cloudy, depending on our state of health.

Other types of colour therapy are where patients are bathed in different coloured lights to help set in motion the healing process, or are sat in rooms with certain types of light to help them recover from illnesses such as seasonal affective disorder (SAD), where they feel depressed and generally under the weather.

Sometimes, just holding a phial of a certain colour, or carrying it around in a handbag or pocket, can subtly work to alter moods for the better.

Theo Gimbel's work on colour therapy, at his well-established Hygeia Studio in Gloucestershire, has shown that certain lights can have a calming effect on body systems, reducing blood pressure and inducing relaxation.

It has been proven scientifically since the last century that colours can have a deep psychological effect on people, and that choice of colours can indicate intricate aspects of personality. The Luscher Colour Test, developed in the 1940s, has been found to be astonishingly accurate in many cases.

The very successful 'Colour Me Beautiful' idea, with its emphasis on 'cool' or 'warm' colours, develops research carried out in Germany during the last century and is, to me, far more than just a matter of wearing the right shades for your skin and hair colouring. I know that since I started wearing my 'right' colours, I have become far more confident and also have much better health.

Irene Bradley, a colour therapist and hypnotherapist, says:

'To me, wearing the right colours was a way of getting myself back into harmony. After a very difficult childhood, and alcoholism in later life, I needed something which was going to make me look good at the same time as feeling good inside.

'I used to wear a lot of black and bright pink, and because of this, looked very tarty. I am very small and blonde, yet I would wear bright red lipstick and tight, low-cut black dresses. I was putting out all these signals and then complaining when men found me sexy or said they were in love with me.

'Now, I never wear any black at all. Since I became a colour analyst I have realised that a lot of people have terrible turmoil inside and that's one reason why they persist in wearing their wrong colours, or colours which make them look ill and tired. Some of my clients won't look at themselves in the mirror – they can't, they hate themselves too much.

'It seems to me that when people have no visual sense, they don't know what they are like inside. Their energy is blocked. Sometimes, I feel that

people need hypnotherapy before they can begin to look at themselves and change the colours they wear. Fair-haired and fair-skinned people who wear a lot of black are trying to blot themselves out: they don't want to be seen.'

Colour analysis and colour therapy can help people to get back in touch with themselves, to harmonise the inner and the outer. It may seem that wearing the 'right' colours is a trivial matter but, like all other aspects of personal growth, it involves taking a close look at oneself and deciding to make changes – never an easy decision.

Information about colour therapy from: Living Colour, 33 Lancaster Grove, London NW3 4EX. Tel: 071–794 1371. **Also**: Hygeia College of Colour Therapy, Brook House, Avening, Tetbury, Glos GL8 8NS. Tel: 0453 832150.

Aura-Soma workshops and colour therapy training: Dev Aura, Little London, Tetford, nr Horncastle, Lincs LN9 6QT. Tel: 0507 533781. **Also**: International Association for Colour Therapy, 73 Elm Bank Gardens, London SW13 0NX.

Dreamwork

Ever since the days of Freud, the interpretation of dreams has become a standard form of psychoanalysis, although we are now fast moving away from the standard Freudian interpretation that everything in dreams has a sexual connotation.

In biblical times, dreams were seen to be forecasting the future: now, they appear to be giving us new interpretations of what happened in the past. If you are interested in interpreting your dreams, to try and discover what your unconscious does when your body is asleep, you should write down your dreams the minute you wake up, and get into the habit of doing this every day. You will most probably find that a pattern emerges, and that interpretation soon becomes possible.

There are very many books available on dream interpretation, but if you have very disturbing or recurring dreams, you may like to consult a therapist who specialises in this kind of work. Sometimes it becomes obvious that a dream is telling you to do something urgently. For about a year before I had therapy to release an obsessive love affair in the past, I had the most extraordinarily vivid dreams about this long-ago love, dreams that were such a potent product of wish fulfilment that I longed for them not to be dreams at all, but reality. As soon as I had dealt with the problem, the dreams disappeared, and I never had another one concerning this person.

Some dream analysts believe that all illnesses and states of mind can be revealed in dreams – if you know how to interpret them.

Information on dream therapy from: Confederation of Healing Organisations, 113 High Street, Berkhamsted, Herts HP4 2DJ. Tel: 0442 870667.

Fasting

Fasting does not sound very pleasant and indeed it is not while you are actually doing it, but it can be a wonderful way of getting to know yourself better, of stilling both the body and mind, and releasing long-held toxins from the body.

Fasting forms an important part of all ancient religions, as it is seen to heighten consciousness. When the body goes without food for a day or two, it's as if another potent anaesthetic is off and you can have mild hallucinations, altered states of consciousness and a feeling of great clarity.

Although some people may have the strength to fast on their own, it is really better to fast under supervision. The Sivananda Yoga Vedanta Centre (see details in *Spiritual Organisations* section) holds regular fasting weekends under supervision, where participants do yoga, go for walks, sleep and rest a lot, and drink weak herb tea all the time. There is also quite a lot of chanting and meditation which, if nothing else, passes the time.

Although at first you may feel quite ill, there will eventually be a tremendous feeling of lightness and clear-headedness, and a wish to continue to eat lightly and abstain from alcohol and heavy, addictive foods. Unfortunately, this feeling soon goes, and before long you'll probably be back to your old ways. You should not fast more than twice a year and, unless you have a medical condition for which fasting is recommended, it should not last for more than a few days.

You will go very quiet, retreat into yourself and not feel like talking too much during the fast. Fasting is, above all, a time for introspection and reflection, and it gives 'time out' from your usual routines and eating patterns. If nothing else, going on a fasting weekend will make you realise just how much energy, time and thought is spent one way or another on food.

Fasting is, of course, one of the standard forms of treatment at nature cure centres and health farms. If you go to a health farm run by naturopaths, you will almost certainly be recommended to fast for a few days.

Information from: Tyringham Naturopathic Clinic, Newport Pagnell, Milton Keynes, Bucks MK16 9ER. Tel: 0908 610450. Fasting, raw food, hydrotheraphy, sauna, jacuzzi, steam bath, acupuncture and massage are offered at this well-established clinic.

Flotation Tanks

Flotation tanks are for some a wonderful experience, whereas other people find them scary. You lie naked (or in a swimsuit) in warm water, totally alone and in the dark while soothing music is played. The idea is that you gradually float away all stress and tension, and emerge relaxed and at ease. It is an experience of total solitude in a soothing and safe environment.

Many health farms and health clubs now have flotation tanks, and a governing body now regulates their use and application.

Information from: Flotation Tank Association, 34 Elms Crescent, London SW4 8QE. Tel: 071–350 1001.

Homoeopathy

Many people's introduction to taking responsibility for their health comes through homoeopathy, the medical treatments which seem to turn science on its head. Homoeopathy, the system of 'like cures like', says that the more diluted a medicine becomes, the more effective it gets.

Homoeopathy was the original 'holistic' treatment as, above all, it seeks to treat the whole person – mind, body, spirit, emotions, as well as bodily complaints. There are literally thousands of homoeopathic medicines available, all of which operate on the principle of setting the body's own self-healing mechanism in motion.

Homoeopathy is widely used for racehorses, which have delicate systems and, recently, trials in France have established that homoeopathic cures can work on humans. Homoeopathy works in the exact opposite way to orthodox or allopathic medicine, which always looks for the antidote, the opposite substance to the disease, as a cure. In homoeopathy, diseases are seen as a 'healing crisis', rather than an enemy to be fought with all the weapons at a doctor's disposal.

Some people's systems respond well to homoeopathic medicines, while others find them completely useless. But, as with so many branches of complementary medicine, the doctor–patient relationship is quite different from that of an ordinary GP. The consultation and case history is lengthy and involved, and the homoeopathic doctor may well ask questions about your personal life, attitudes, family, personality type and so on.

Information on qualified homoeopaths from: Institute of Complementary Medicine (see page 143) or The British Homoeopathic Association, 27a Devonshire Place, London W1N 1RJ. Tel: 071–935 2136.

Hypnotherapy

Hypnotherapy, originally used by Freud and then abandoned, is making a big comeback, as it is often a far quicker way of uncovering buried and repressed memories than standard psychoanalysis or psychotherapy. It is also extremely useful for overcoming habits such as smoking and nailbiting – but only if, deep down, you really want to relinquish the habit.

Hypnosis is used for past-life and regression therapy, and is now seen as highly respectable. Many people still worry that all kinds of untoward suggestions will be made to them while they are under hypnosis, but this is unlikely, if not impossible.

Information from: British Society of Hypnotherapists, 38 Orbain Road, London SW6 7JZ. Tel: 071–385 1166.

Laughter Clinics

The idea that smiling and laughter can promote health was first researched in America, where it was found that when we smile, this activates neurotransmitters in the brain which affect all bodily functions to their betterment. Conversely, if we scowl or look angry, body systems are alerted, blood pressure goes up and the heart starts racing.

This happens even when we don't actually feel the emotions connected with looking happy, sad, angry and so on, but merely contort our faces into expressions associated with these emotions.

The reasons why smiling and laughter aid healing are complex, but have to do with being cheerful and positive – a potent message that runs through the whole personal growth movement. Humans are the only creatures possessing the ability to laugh and smile – in spite of some dog owners swearing that their dogs laugh at jokes – and although laughter has been called the best medicine for centuries, science is only now beginning to be able to tell us why.

It seems that smiling and laughter powerfully reduce stress and, just as negative emotions can make us ill, positive emotions can make us better. In America, there are now several laughter clinics in hospitals for AIDS and cancer patients and, in the UK, laughter clinics are now being set up on the NHS. The value of laughter as a healing tool is well established in France, where professional laughers will come to your home, and enable you to forget all your cares and worries through laughter.

But you don't have to go to a clinic to gain the healing benefits of laughing. Whenever you can see the funny side of a situation, you are protecting your health.

Information on laughter workshops and clinics: The British Holistic Medical Association, 179 Gloucester Place, London NW1 6DX. Tel: 071–262 5299.

Matthew Manning Healing Centre

Matthew Manning, born in 1955, has established himself as one of the leading healers in Britain. His abilities have been closely investigated by many scientists and he genuinely does seem able to affect body cells to their betterment.

In recent years, Matthew has turned his attentions to self-healing, as he believes this is what all effective healing is.

Starting from small beginnings, his healing centre is now one of the busiest in the country, and has become a big-business venture. He is usually fully booked for months, but runs courses and workshops at a number of venues teaching self-healing and the meaning of illness. All of us, Manning believes, have the power to heal, both ourselves and others.

Information from: Matthew Manning Healing Centre, 39 Abbeygate St, Bury St Edmunds IP33 1LW. Tel: 0248 830222.

Neuro-Linguistic Programming

NLP was developed in the early 1970s in America and is rapidly establishing itself as *the* therapy of the 1990s. With NLP, the therapist closely monitors each client, noting every action, the way they look, respond to questions, whether they use eye contact and so on. From this, a picture of the client and his or her needs is gradually built up, and each client is treated as a completely different entity, unlike in some branches of psychotherapy, which look for set patterns and explanations.

NLP uses mirroring and matching techniques, where the therapist closely matches the body language of the client, and the emphasis is on recalling good feelings, so that these can gradually replace the unpleasant ones, and become uppermost in the client's memory. The emphasis all the time is on replacing bad with good, so that eventually a more positive, harmonious attitude can be gained. NLP is most often taught in groups, and clients can become their own therapists, although groups must be led by a fully qualified NLP therapist, as the technique is highly skilled.

Information from: Association for Neuro-linguistic Programming, 100b Carysfort Road, London N16 9AP. Tel: 071–241 3664.

Also: British Hypnosis Research, 8 Paston Place, Brighton BN2 1HA. Tel: 0273 693622, offer a one-year, part-time training course in NLP. Entry requirements are an established career and formal qualifications in one of the caring professions; or a first degree in an academic subject.

Past-Life Therapy

This is rapidly becoming one of the most popular of all healing therapies. Although small numbers of people have been carrying out past-life therapy for very many years – one of the first was psychiatrist Denys Kelsey, who was married to the past-life novelist Joan Grant – it is only since the late 1980s that this type of therapy has come out into the open.

Detractors maintain that we can never know whether a 'past life' is imagination, remembering something we have read or seen in a film, or trying to please the therapist. Apart from which, very many people in the West do not believe in past incarnations, even though this is central to the religious beliefs of most Eastern religions.

But you do not have to believe in past lives for the therapy to work. Those who specialise in this type of therapy say that it can be used to address problems which seem to have no cause in the present, such as phobias about flying, water, spiders and so on – objects or activities which have never done the patient any harm in this life.

Most past-life therapists use a kind of hypnosis to regress the patient, and then, in this state of altered consciousness, the patient begins to reveal a life which may have caused the problem. This kind of therapy can be used for all kinds of difficulties in the present, to sort out relationships, come to terms with parental abuse, or discover one's true vocation.

Past-life therapist Roger Woolger, a Jungian psychoanalyst, has found that it works far better than standard analysis, as it produces quicker and more far-reaching results.

Information from: Morning Light Healing Centre (address in *Spiritual Organisations* section) who offer past-life therapy. **Also**: Dr Francesca Rossetti, Flat 5, 41 Lansdowne Road, London W11 2LQ. Tel: 071–792 2957.

Rebirthing

Considered by some to be the archetypal New Age therapy, rebirthing takes you back to the moment of your birth and invites you to relieve the experience. The concept behind rebirthing is that many neuroses, fears and difficulties may have set in with birth, and these have somehow become embedded in our system over the years, causing us to function less than optimally.

Rebirthing techniques developed from the work of Arthur Janov, of primal therapy fame, who believed that birth traumas are often held in the body for very many years, and can contribute to psychological and relationship problems in later life.

If you know you had a difficult birth, you may be interested in trying the rebirthing technique. In the past, LSD was often used to activate the part of the mind which could remember birth; now deep breathing techniques are used by most rebirthers.

Some therapists believe that many chronic health problems, such as migraine, asthma and certain phobias, may be caused by birth trauma. When this trauma is relived, it can then be released harmlessly, and the way cleared for better physical and emotional health.

Information from: The British Rebirth Society, 18 Woodfield Road, Redland, Bristol BS6 6JQ.

Reflexology

Also known as zone therapy, reflexology is a method of healing whereby the soles of the feet are manipulated, in the belief that this can stimulate and activate sluggish organs. According to reflexologists, every area on the foot corresponds to a particular body organ.

The hands can also be used for this treatment, although it is more common to massage the soles of the feet.

Although it sounds a gentle therapy, reflexology can be surprisingly painful when tender spots are touched. Usually, treatment continues until the area is no longer painful, as this means the organ has now been healed. As a form of alternative healing, it has gained great respectability over the past few years, and is widely available. Reflexology can also be used as a diagnostic tool, and although practitioners are often not medically qualified, they will usually have undergone a course of training in this therapy.

Information on courses and practitioners from: The Bayly School of Reflexology, Monks Orchard, Whitbourne, Worcester WR6 5RB. Tel: 0886 21207.

Relaxation Therapy

It is impossible to be truly well when you are under stress. Most of us want to relax – yet we can't. There is far more to relaxation than slumping in front of the television or lying on a warm beach.

Genuine relaxation takes great concentration, as every muscle, nerve and joint has to be relaxed in turn. For many people it has to be learned, and it can be a useful first step towards stilling the mind and being able to listen to that important inner voice which is at the heart of personal growth.

People who find it difficult to relax and would like to learn how to do it, can contact: Stresswise, Dept of Biological Sciences, John Dalton Building, Manchester University, Manchester M1 5GD. This Centre offers relaxation training, and maybe able to put you in touch with a centre that is local to you.

Shamanism

In ancient cultures, shamans were both priests and healers, people who were able to go into a state of altered consciousness or trance, and who were considered to have magical powers.

Modern shamans are people who are able, it is said, to get in touch with spirit guides from other realms. There were many such shamans in the early days of the Findhorn Foundation, people who communicated with nature spirits. This still goes on at Findhorn, and may contribute to the powerful atmosphere there.

Shamanism is now being used to help ordinary people to get in touch with their own 'spirit guides', and other states of reality. As such, modern psychological techniques are used, as well as ancient ritual, divination, and traditional medicine such as herbalism and prayer wheels. In some schools of shamanism, headphones and other items of high-tech electronic gear are used to aid altered consciousness, and an awareness of the spiritual realms.

An introduction to modern shamanism is offered at: Eagle's Wing Centre for Contemporary Shamanism, 58 Westbere Road, London NW2 3RU. Tel: 071–435 8174.

Sound Therapy

The therapeutic benefits of music and singing are only just being realised. All too often, we are stopped from singing when we are at primary school, as we are told we sing out of tune. We then become so nervous of people hearing us when we sing that we never open our mouths in song again.

Teacher and healer Chris James, a big, burly Australian, is convinced that we all have beautiful voices, and that we only need to realise it. His belief is that we can reclaim our own power through the joy of singing.

Chanting, used by most Eastern religions, has long been known to have a powerful effect on the mind and body. If chants are continued for long enough, they can profoundly alter consciousness. The vibrations can have an effect on the heartbeat and blood pressure, and prolonged chanting can bring about a trance state where heightened insights and perceptions become possible.

Chanting can be seen as a way of stilling the mind, stopping the constant traffic which is often counter-productive, and giving the mind a rest, a chance to think straight and direct the thoughts.

Psychiatrist John Diamond, who has pioneered music therapy in Australia, believes that certain types of music have a dramatic effect on body systems, whether or not we 'like' the actual sounds. He believes one important aspect is the intention of the composer. The less ego, the more healing a piece of music is likely to be. In particular, he believes, medieval Gregorian chants have powerful healing benefits.

Information on Chris James's workshops: New Life Designs, Arnica House, 170 Campden Hill Road, London W8 7AS. Tel: 071–938 3788.

The London Voice Centre: 30 Redchurch St, London E2 7DP. Tel: 071–613 1636.

Inner Sound and Voice (ancient chanting techniques): 9 Yonge Park, London N4 3NU. Tel: 071–607 5819.

Spiritual Healing

Many people are confused by spiritual healing. Is it faith healing, do the healers get in touch with spirits, what happens? In fact, spiritual healing can be explained very simply: it is the channelling of some kind of healing energy which transmits itself from the healer to the patient. Most spiritual healers believe that the healing power comes through them, rather than from them.

Spiritual healing is now attracting scientific research, and scientists have been able to show that such healers do have some kind of 'power', by undertaking experiments with plants – entities not readily subject to the power of suggestion. It has been conclusively demonstrated that healers have the ability to make plants grow faster, as has been shown in several controlled experiments, both in Britain and America.

Spiritual healing is mainly used nowadays in conjunction with orthodox medical treatments, rather than as a substitute for them. It often happens that people become healers when they have had a positive experience of spiritual healing themselves. It seems that most of us do have a healing gift, to some extent at least, but that like all other gifts and talents, it is more pronounced in some people than others. Also, it improves with practice.

Most people who have opened up their minds to spiritual healing discover that it leads to a greater understanding of the healing process, and a willingness to take on board the possibility of clairvoyance, telepathy, reincarnation and karma.

Information from: The National Federation of Spiritual Healers, Old Manor Farm Studio, Church Street, Sunbury-on-Thames, Middlesex TW16 6RG. Tel: 0932 783164.

Tai Chi Chuan

Tai Chi consists of a number of graceful, flowing movements which are designed to bring the body, spirit and emotions into harmony. Although often bracketed with martial arts, Tai Chi is really designed for relaxation and concentration rather than self-defence.

The right sort of breathing is important to make the movements, and you do not have to be strong or fit. The idea is that through the right kind of movement, energy, or *chi*, is released through the body.

Nowadays, Tai Chi is often recommended to people who suffer from stress, tension and anxiety, and it can be a wonderful way to unwind after a heavy day's work. It is not competitive, and there is no winning or losing. It is good for lowering high blood pressure.

Information from: The British Tai Chi Association, 7 Upper Wimpole Street, London W1M 7TD. Tel: 071–935 8444.

Touch for Health (Applied Kinesiology)

This is a hands-on therapy which involves touching various muscles to see whether they are performing properly, or are suffering from some kind of dysfunction.

It is used as a diagnostic technique to indicate imbalance and weakness in the muscles, and stimulate the flow of energy through the meridians, or acupuncture points. Thus this, in common with so many complementary therapies, glances towards ancient Eastern healing arts.

Today, kinesiology is most often used to diagnose food allergies, and to suggest healthier dietary alternatives.

Information from: Academy of Systematic Kinesiology, 39 Browns Road, Surbiton, Surrey KT5 8ST. Tel: 081–399 3215.

Also: The Aetherius Society, 757 Fulham Road, London SW6 5UU, tel: 071–736 4187, uses and teaches kinesiology to test food allergies and other health imbalances.

Yoga for Health

Yoga is now often seen as a form of keep-fit, but in recent years it has also been closely investigated for its health-giving properties. In particular, yogic breathing, known as pranayama, can reduce asthma, diabetes and other chronic complaints. So far, no similar trials have been carried out for postural, or hatha, yoga.

The Yoga for Health Foundation in Bedfordshire is a residential centre where people can go to recover their health through yoga. The emphasis is on personal development through breathing and physical postures.

The Foundation specialises in recuperative holidays for those suffering from multiple sclerosis, a condition which usually gradually disables, but which can be kept at bay, some people believe, with evening primrose oil, the right kind of exercise and a positive attitude.

Information from: The Yoga for Health Foundation, Ickwell Bury, Biggleswade, Bedfordshire SG18 9EF. Tel: 0767 27271.

Also: British Wheel of Yoga, 1 Hamilton Place, Sleaford, Lincs NG34 7ES. Tel: 0529 306851.

Iyengar Yoga Institute: 223a Randolph Avenue, London W9 1NL. Tel: 071–624 3080.

Note: this section on healing treatments is not definitive: there are so many therapies these days, with more coming into being all the time, that it would take a book the size of a telephone directory just to mention them all. Readers who wish to make sure they are contacting a properly-qualified practitioner in the therapy that interests them can contact the Institute for Complementary Medicine (see address on page 143.)

The ICM has now investigated, and can give details on: aromatherapy, homoeopathy, acupuncture, reflexology – where certain pressure points on the foot are activated to generate health throughout the whole body – spiritual healing, chiropractic and osteopathy, kinesiology and therapeutic massage.

Although not exactly a formal governing body, the ICM has been investigating complementary medicine for nearly two decades, and has information on accredited training courses, for those who may wish to train as a complementary therapist.

For information on counselling and psychotherapy, contact: The British Association for Counselling, 1 Regent Place, Rugby CV21 2PJ. Tel: 0788 578328. Their yearly handbook, available from public libraries, gives lists of accredited counsellors and training courses all over the UK.

Chapter 7

Warnings

Are 'they' out to get you?

An overwhelming fear that many people have is that groups and organis-ations are basically cults, out to get you in their net like a spider, so that you will never be free again. It is certainly true that some pseudo-religious organisations are cults, are dangerous and *are* out to get you.

But they are not in the majority. The whole New Age movement is not one giant plot to get everybody in the clutches of some charismatic movement from which they will never be able to extricate themselves.

By far the great majority of those offering courses, seminars and workshops are people who have themselves had some kind of awakening, which they now want to pass on to others. Of course, there will be charges for these courses, which may be either hidden or up front. In some cases, you may be asked to make a donation, while in others, there will be set charges. Usually, these are reasonable for what is on offer and nobody is making a vast fortune.

Certainly, most complementary healers are not making anything like the kind of money that an average country GP would make.

The real problem, as I see it, is that most human beings are flawed, just as we are ourselves. This means that there should never be over-reliance on any one method or movement. They should be seen, rather, as stepping-stones, lending a helping hand and should never create dependence.

On the other hand, do not be taken in by any hard-sell methods, cold calling, 'special offers' or attempts to drag you in off the street to sample personality testing, telling your future or any other seductive trick.

It should always be you, not they, who makes the decision to join a particular organisation, or attend a seminar or workshop.

Then, only go along with a particular organisation or movement *while you feel you are gaining benefit*. This is most important. With some, you will benefit for perhaps a very short time, with others, maybe not at all. But in the mean time you will have checked out the organisation and your own attitude towards it.

One reason why some people become New Age junkies is because they have gained benefit from one or more activities, courses or groups, and want to improve and increase this benefit. So, they are constantly trying new things. For some, this can become a bit of an addictive fix, but it often happens that when there is an improvement in one area, you want to improve all the other areas of your life.

In some ways, this can be likened to doing up a house. If you move into a house where every room needs decorating, there will be an enormous, visible difference when even one room is done. You then can't wait to get the others done. Gradually, as more of the house is done up, all the bits that are not done up will seem even grottier by contrast.

If you start by changing your diet, you may then move on from wanting to become physically fit, to wanting to become mentally and emotionally fit. There are no limits to personal growth – there's always a little corner somewhere that could do with brightening up. Also, you have to keep on the move.

You may one day outgrow something which seemed satisfying and all-pervading at one stage in your growth journey. So, there is nothing wrong with investigating new movements, new organisations, new ways of self-help. Some will work for you, some won't.

But don't worry that the whole growth area is littered with charlatans and quacks. These do exist, of course, but their influence is usually short-lasting and they are very soon found out.

Specific warnings

There are some obvious signs which should alert you to the spurious organisations.

1 An impossibly luxurious lifestyle on the part of the founder of the organisation. Obviously, we all have to have a roof over our heads, and when you have given up your job to run a growth movement, you need to retain an income. But there is a big difference between charging, say, £300 for a weekend seminar in a hotel, and asking you to 'donate' several thousand pounds for the good of the organisation, and the good of your soul.

It's one thing to be businesslike; another to leave you without an income so that you will come to rely completely on the organisation.

People who are genuinely interested in helping others to grow, usually because they have had some kind of special awakening themselves, are non-egotistical, not interested in the outward trappings of power and success, or in making vast sums of money for themselves. While there is nothing wrong with enjoying a comfortable lifestyle, it is obscene to have ninety or so Rolls-Royces, as Bhagwan Shree Rajneesh did at the height of his success in the West.

2 Super-charisma. Beware any leader of a supposed growth organisation who tells you that having sex with him is part of your growth pattern, or who wants you to change your name or give up your job to follow him and his organisation. I say 'him' because, according to my researches, all the self-styled gurus who have acted in this manner have been male.

3 Equally, be on your guard with any organisation which seems just too poor or too unsuccessful. Because, if they can't get themselves together, how are they going to be able to advise anybody else? Always look closely at the other disciples and followers of any movement or organisation and ask yourself: do they seem genuinely happier, in charge of their lives, nicer, more intelligent people than the usual? If so, then they are their own best advertisement. Otherwise, you would do well to leave them alone.

To sum up, if you are interested in the sound of any movement, you should be looking for efficiency and pleasantness in all dealings; reasonable sums charged, neither too excessive nor too tiny; prompt replies to answerphone messages, letters and enquiries, a pleasant, always courteous manner; literate and well-written information material; a clear indication of the costs involved; and a willingness to answer any questions concerning the activities and scope of the organisation.

YOU should be the one who makes all the running – they should not come after you. So, if any organisation pesters you on the phone, calls round to your house when you have specifically asked them not to, uses questionable recruiting techniques (or, indeed, *any* recruiting techniques) or behaves in any way that makes you feel uncomfortable, make your excuses and leave. If you ever get the feeling that they need you more than you need them, don't have anything to do with them.

Never ever pledge anything, either money or services, until you are absolutely sure of the level to which you want to become involved. There should not be any pressure on you to sign binding documents.

The material and literature should be fairly glossy – smart enough to look efficient and effective, but not so glossy as to invite comments about where the money has come from to produce such literature.

Only go along with the things that you personally like, and which make you feel comfortable and at ease. A feeling of unease should be your sign that a particular organisation is not the right one for you.

Chapter 8

Conclusion

When you embark on a journey of personal growth, you start to see everything through a completely different pair of glasses. It's as if you have taken off the dark sunglasses and put on a pair of powerful specs that enable you to see everything with super-clarity. What was dim before now grows bright, what was hidden now becomes apparent.

It's not that the world has changed – *you* have changed, wonderfully, and for the better. And as you go on, ever more insights, ever more revelations, come to you so that, eventually, everything falls into place.

You will discover that all your relationships – with yourself, your partner, your children, your workmates, your neighbours, and even your cat and your houseplants – can undergo a dramatic improvement.

No longer will you blame people for not being what you expected them to be, for not being perfect. You will learn that the only real way to regard other humans, whatever your relationship with them, is with detached love. You will come to see them as people who are separate from yourself, not extensions.

It will become obvious that the only person you have the power to change is yourself. You cannot inspire, teach or instruct anybody else, except by your example. It will also become clear that the way you see the world and your place in it depends on your own consciousness and beliefs. There is no objective, ultimate reality in the world – only ways of looking at things. And if you look at the world with kindness, compassion and love – that's what you will get back from it.

Conclusion

This is not to say, of course, that you will lose all your judgement and discrimination, and henceforth see everything through rose-tinted glasses. Of course you will still be aware of monstrous injustices, cruelty and unfairness. The difference is that you will be able to see it all at a distance, as a comedy or tragedy that is being played out on the world stage.

But it won't make you personally angry any more.

You will now find it easy to be cheerful, and you will be able to regard every experience in life as a learning experience, rather than as 'good' or 'bad'. You will discover a new compassion, a new empathy with others, and be able to see that they are doing their best. If they could do any better, they would.

You will cease to become angry at others' real or imagined shortcomings, and there will no longer be paranoia, phobias or timidity. You will lose all the fear you may previously have had about other people. You will not fear rapists, muggers, kidnappers or burglars, or expect that people are lying in wait to do you down at every turn.

You will no longer be willing to give away your power to others, to try and make them responsible for your actions. You will no longer blame 'them' for high taxation or unjust laws, but see that we have all played our part, whether this is through anger, apathy or resentment.

You will come to take responsibility for your physical, emotional and mental health, and realise that you are your own expert, your own guru. You will realise that although others may be able to guide and inform you up to a point, they cannot do your growing for you.

You will find that you are blessed with new insights, new creativity as less energy is taken up with blame and recrimination. You will start to make connections, to see the essential harmony and wholeness of everything. Life will no longer seem random and chaotic, and everything that happens will come to be seen as a jewelled movement, fitting in perfectly.

You will find that you start to spread radiance around you, that people seem to come alive in your company and want to be with you. You will never lack for friends. As a bonus, your health and looks will improve, and you will most probably find that, as well as everything else, the path to personal growth is a highly rejuvenating one.

Because anger, hostility and resentment will gradually vanish from your thoughts, your face will start to reduce its lines and wrinkles.

Nothing will bother you so much any more. You will be able to accept change in your life, come to see that nothing is necessarily permanent and that few things stay the same for very long. You will have acquired the resilience to cope with change, and be able to welcome it as a new experience.

One of the most wonderful insights will be that nobody else can make you happy or, conversely, make you miserable. You will acquire such inward strength that other people cannot disturb your equanimity. Emotional dependency on other people will vanish, as you become strong in your own right.

As time goes on, you will find that you no longer want to abuse your body. You won't want to smoke, you won't want to drink so much that you get hangovers, and you will probably become far more careful about what foods you are prepared to put into your body. Many people decide to become vegetarian when they begin their journey of self-transformation. In fact, changing diet is for many people a starting point for their personal growth.

You will be less inclined to eat foods that come to you as the result of cruelty. Factory farming will seem abhorrent, and you will not want to support this industry by eating its products.

You will become more careful with your money. That doesn't mean that you will become stingy, but you will see money as energy, as a resource which enables you to buy the goods that you want. Now that you are no longer frittering money away on goods or enterprises that are essentially worthless, or give no pleasure or satisfaction, you will find you have more money to spend, that it goes further. You will not want to waste, but to husband your resources.

You will become more adept at getting your own needs met, rather than trying to meet those of other people – which is impossible anyway.

The need for romantic entanglements or addictive relationships will also fall away as they are replaced by relationships which are mutually supportive and enhancing. You will not need anybody, nor will they need you. You will stop worrying about other people and what they might do, realising that worry doesn't make the slightest difference to the outcome.

You will become more assertive, realising that you are as important as anybody else on this planet, and that you do not need to defer to anybody. At the same time, you will treat people with respect and trust – in the way that you would like to be treated yourself.

You will no longer be causing sorrow to other people, upsetting them, or making them cross or angry to get a reaction. You will be able to consider your words before you speak them. There will be an end to self-sabotage as you are able to direct your energies only towards those activities which are directly going to nurture and sustain you.

Conclusion

You will come to realise that there is always a choice, that although we cannot always select our circumstances, we are able to choose our attitude. You will learn the difference between according everybody love and positivity, and being a doormat, and come to realise that the two could not be more different.

Because you have self-respect, you will be able to accord this to others, to see everybody else as full human beings, rather than as a wife, mother, brother, sister, black person, white person, disabled person, old person. You will be able to stop seeing people purely in terms of their roles, and start to see them as human beings first, with exactly the same range of emotions, fears, doubts and hopes that you have yourself.

You will be able to replace wishful thinking, hoping and praying by a strong belief in yourself.

If this all sounds wonderful, it is. These are all the things I have learned through my own journey of personal growth and, although at times it was painful to lay the old aside, there is no doubt that the journey has been worth it. Not that it has finished, by any means – I know there is still a long way to go. But there is never the feeling now of being caught up in random, meaningless events over which I have little choice or control.

I've learned that I have an amazing amount of choice in my life. I can choose whether or not to work, and how much to work. Of course, the less work I do, the less money I'm likely to earn – then I have to weigh up the pros and cons of having more time to myself against less money to spend. I've learned that I can choose where I live, that I can choose my friends and acquaintances.

I can choose to be by myself or with other people. I can choose to have good relationships with everybody I meet, and not alienate them through bitterness, anger, or shows of superiority or envy. I've learned that it's good for me to be able to share in the success of others, rather than to feel jealous because they seem to be more successful than me in some ways.

There are, as I hope this book has made clear, very many routes towards effective self-transformation. For most of us, some significant event will trigger off the search. Very often, the growth process comes as a surprise. We will have some kind of revelation, find that we are suddenly able to kick a habit which previously was stronger than we were, or a serious or debilitating illness will provide us with a chance to look inwards, to ask questions that we never asked before.

Growth cannot be forced. Always, it starts when you are ready for it, when life events urge you at last to look at where you are going.

If there is one important message to be learned from the whole field of personal growth it is that we should never feel that any event is 'terrible'. All pain, all suffering, provides a chance for growth, although this does not mean you have to be in dreadful physical or emotional pain before the growth process can start. Sometimes the veil is drawn aside easily, sometimes there has to be an almighty tug.

As we are all individuals, so the starting point, and the growth process, will be different for each one of us. But for each of us, it will be appropriate.

Here are some case histories of ordinary people who found very different routes to self-awareness and growth.

Alison discovered that being able to give up smoking gave her the courage and confidence to make decisions and choices that previously seemed beyond her. She said:

'I had been a chain-smoker for more than twenty years, and never ever thought I'd be able to give it up. Every time I tried, my then husband said to me: you'll never do it – and I believed him

'It was only when, after a very great effort and determination to prove him wrong, I managed to become a non-smoker, that I was actually able to look at various aspects of my life. It seemed to me then that I had always allowed myself to be under the shadow of men. That revelation came to me with amazing clarity once I had stopped smoking.

'I had wanted to go to university, but my domineering father considered it was a waste of time and money for a girl. Instead of defying him, as I could have done, because grants were available in those days as they are now, I never went. I simply fulfilled his low expectations of me by getting married at the first opportunity, before I had qualified for any job or profession whatever.

'I then had three children in quick succession, without ever stopping to think what I was doing. I think now that to chain-smoke was a way of covering up deep unhappiness and disappointment at myself. I felt powerless and, in a way, smoking seemed the only thing I could choose to do. Of course, gradually, smoking took away what little confidence I had because I became completely dependent on it. I had allowed men to dominate me; now I was allowing smoking to dominate me.

'In my marriage, I had chosen an older, dominating type of man, similar to my father. I suppose I thought that's what men were. But when I managed to give up, I was able to take stock of my entire life. It was as if a dark cloud had rolled away.

'I felt suddenly free, and independent. I realised that my marriage was over, that it had actually been over for many years but I was too nervous to branch out on my own. I knew I would never flourish in the relationship, but never having earned my own living, I didn't know how I would manage.

'But after stopping smoking, I was able to stand up to my husband, and tell him I wanted to leave him. It was a very difficult divorce, as he didn't want to cope with the loss of status that it would involve, or losing the house. I used the money gained from the sale of our large house to buy myself a small cottage, and, for the first time in my life, had a bit of capital of my own.

'I'd always wanted to write, but never had the confidence. I booked up a residential writing course, and was astonished when the tutor said I had real skill.' [*Alison has now written five novels, and is financially independent.*] 'But more important than that is that I've come to realise that I am responsible for myself, that nobody else is responsible for me, and that I can make choices which nourish me and enable me to continue my growth, rather than stifle it, as before.

'When I was married, I would never have considered going for aromatherapy, meditation or Alexander technique classes, all of which I do now. It would have seemed terrible to spend time and money on myself. Deep down, I didn't think I was worth it. Now, I have come to realise that when I do things for me, rather than trying to please other people, which is an illusion anyway, I actually do spread happiness. There's no point in trying to cater for other people's needs if you are seething with resentment inside, as I've discovered. Before, I used to think I had to put other people first.

'In fact, I was just wiping myself out, and doing nobody any good. But I'm sure none of these revelations would have been vouchsafed to me if I hadn't managed to gain power over my addiction first.'

Sidney had always considered himself a rational, scientific sort of person. He'd never had even the slightest interest in looking inwards, and was certainly not contemplating any kind of religious conversion. He'd given all that sort of thing up without regret when he left his local church as a teenager. For most of his adult life he had considered himself an atheist.

He was working as the science editor of a national newspaper, when a contact of his asked if he was interested in going to a science evening hosted by the Brahma Kumaris Spiritual University.

'I'd never heard of these people. I was very reluctant to go along and even when I'd agreed, I kept thinking that I would find a very good excuse not to turn up.

'My contact, who was a leading exponent of the new physics, was going to be a speaker at this event, but I could easily have fixed up another meeting with him. I asked him whether there was going to be any meditation or chanting or any of that nonsense, and he said no, it was going to be a perfectly normal evening.

'Well, when I got there I'd never seen anything so weird. There were these smiling Indian women, dressed in white saris, who seemed to be beings from another planet. They wafted round with glasses of orange and apple juice, and I thought: what have I let myself in for? I felt acutely uncomfortable, and even more so when, after we all sat down waiting for the talks to begin, one of the women announced there would be a few minutes of silent meditation.

'I sat there staring into space, waiting for it all to be over. Then it happened. I began to see an aura, a kind of halo, around the elderly Indian lady who was leading the meditation. Suddenly, I was transported, quite against my conscious will, into another world. It was like the most absolute bliss, far greater than sex, more wonderful than the most wonderful meal, amazing scenery, or ecstatic good news.

'I felt I had to get to the bottom of it and, afterwards, I booked up a meditation course with this movement. It was all so much unlike anything I had done before that I could hardly believe it. But every time, during meditation, the same thing happened – I was transported into another world of bliss. It still seemed to me that the teachings were utter nonsense; they went completely against my scientific training and beliefs, and didn't fit into any of my existing beliefs. I learned about karma, reincarnation, time being circular instead of linear – and it all seemed to me so much unscientific rubbish.

'But, in the end, because of the experiences during meditation, which could not be denied, my life was changed completely. For the first time, everything began to fall into place. I learned that modern science and ancient religions were actually saying much the same things, and that in fact, the teachings I was hearing made complete logical sense. I just had to make some adjustments to my own way of thinking.

'Gradually, my attitude towards myself and other people improved out of all recognition. I realised that, previously, I had always been under great stress, whatever job I had been in. All my jobs seemed to take a lot out of me. I had thought that this was because of the demands of the job, but I came to realise that it was because of my own fears. I was terrified of not being thought good or conscientious enough, and I wanted all my editors and fellow workers to love me. So I worked myself into the ground.

'There was also a lot of ego involved. I had to keep getting the biggest, the best, stories – and I hated it when a colleague got a bigger byline, or a better story. Practising meditation gave me valuable time out from that stress, and made me able to start pacing myself sensibly. I think now that the reason I had such blissful experiences during meditation was because I so much needed to still my mind.

'I believe now that if I'd gone on as before I would have had a heart attack, or at least a serious illness. But as I became more peaceful in myself, my health improved and so did all my relationships with other people. I was no longer so paranoid – a consequence, I'm sure, of the utter exhaustion I was so often in. When I went on holiday, I would usually go down with a cold, or flu for the first few days. It was such a regular occurrence that I'm sure it was a consequence of rushing around so much in the job. I also realised that my exhaustion was self-imposed, rather than being forced on my by uncaring bosses in a highly competitive and ruthless industry.

'Now, when I go into work, people are amazed at how peaceful and serene I am, even when under great pressure. It's so unlike how I was before – hyperactive, frenetic, always in a tearing hurry, always late, always overstretched.

'For me, though, the meditation could never have worked just by itself. It had to be acompanied by a world view which satisfied me intellectually. All my awkward questions had to be answered to my satisfaction – it wasn't enough just to be bathed in a sea of bliss and altered consciousness. I now find that I can combine meditation perfectly well with my work, and that it enhances, rather than decreases, the quality and quantity of my output.

'I know that a lot of people are nervous of meditation because they fear it will make them lose their sharp edge, their competitive spirit. I've certainly acquired a different attitude to work, in that it is no longer quite so all-important to my life, but I feel I have put it in its place. Before, it was addictive and I was powerless over it. Now, I realise that it had the power to destroy me, and I am working just as effectively without that nervewracking addiction.

'Now, whenever things aren't going well at work, or when I'm tussling with a difficult story, I spend a few moments in silent meditation. At first, my colleagues laughed at me and called me 'The Saint', but they can see what a difference it's made to my life. Also, I'm no longer a heavy drinker, as before, as I've found that alcohol interferes with my ability to meditate – and that I'd rather have the clarity that comes from meditation than the fog which results from over-indulgence in alcohol. So another happy consequence is that I'm no longer in danger of becoming an old soak.'

For Carol, the route to self-transformation came through a diagnosis of breast cancer – not perhaps the starting-point that most people would want to choose. Carol said:

'I'd just been through a horribly painful divorce, where I thought I'd behaved exceptionally well. I had never wanted to get divorced at all, but my then husband announced he'd fallen in love with somebody else, and was going to leave me.

'It wasn't long after that that I developed breast cancer. I was sure the two events were related but the doctors at the hospital I went to said no, there was no evidence that divorce caused breast cancer. I had a biopsy, then a lumpectomy, but the cancer wasn't cured.

'In the end, determined to fight it, I went to the Bristol Cancer Help Centre. There, I found such a different approach that I could hardly believe it. There was meditation, relaxation, guided visualisation, group therapy, a new approach to diet, music and art therapy – all the things that nourished people and made them feel important, rather than just a tumour in a certain area. Through going to Bristol, I was able to face up to my life and realise why I had developed breast cancer.

'It seemed to me, looking back, that I had always been the sort of person who seemed sweet and accommodating on the surface, but seethed with resentment just below. I know I allowed people to walk all over me. I had let my husband go with hardly a murmur, blamed myself for not being attractive enough, sexy enough, or interested enough in his welfare. If I'd been a different kind of wife, I used to tell myself, he might have stayed.

'When I went to Bristol, I was able to face up to these feelings and realise that I had been sabotaging myself over the years, putting myself down, telling myself that what happened to me didn't matter. But if I was to have a chance of getting better, I had to star in my own life.

'It was the first time I'd ever really concentrated on myself. And as I came to learn these important lessons about myself, the tumour shrank and then disappeared. The reason it has gone, I'm sure, is because I have now learned the lessons that the cancer was trying to teach me. I don't think, either, that it will come back. I feel I can say that with complete confidence, because I am such a different person to how I used to be.

'A lot of people have poured scorn on the Bristol approach, saying that it's bad enough having cancer in the first place without blaming yourself for it into the bargain. But, taking responsibility for yourself isn't by any means the same as blaming yourself. I have faced up to my cancer, looked after myself instead of passively putting myself in the hands of the doctors, who don't actually know me at all – and I have come out a winner.

'Before having cancer, I never even thought about personal growth. Even if I'd heard the term, it would have meant nothing whatever to me. For me, it took a brush with death to make me understand just how very important it is for all of us to pay attention to our own needs, and look after our own health in body, mind and spirit. My illness also helped me to realise that physical illnesses never happen in isolation, but are a response to the system being under severe stress. They always happen for a reason – to get us to look at ourselves. I'm sure now that emotional stress is the biggest single cause of serious disease.'

For many years, Jim had suffered from chronic migraines. They were so bad that he often had to go to bed for a day or two, and lie in a darkened room. He had tried all the orthodox medical treatments, also acupuncture, homoeopathy, relaxation, but nothing seemed to make any difference for long. In the end, Jim's doctor gave him phials of a powerful drug which had to be injected when the pain got beyond bearing.

This drug was to be used only in emergencies, as it knocked out half of his brain, so that he could not concentrate on even the simplest thing. It was a drastic solution, and not really the answer.

One day, there was a notice at Jim's health centre which announced that a spiritual healer was going to come in one day a week as part of the surgery's health promotion plan. Jim went to see the healer who, to Jim's surprise, was a middle-aged man much like himself, not particularly educated or erudite. In fact, the healer had been a policeman before discovering a healing gift in himself. Jim, a carpenter, said:

'I was extremely sceptical. I didn't expect anything to happen, but the migraines were getting so bad I was prepared to try anything. As the healer gently put his hands on my head, I could feel a kind of intense heat penetrating right through my skull. It was weird. It was the most wonderful sensation, and the best way I can describe it was as if love was transmitting itself right through my body.

'Immediately after that one session, the migraines began to get better. I had six healing sessions in all, and for three years now, I have not had a single migraine. After all the years of torment, it was a true miracle.

'But the greatest miracle of all was that the healer told me I had a healing gift as well. I didn't believe it, of course, but I thought I'd try it out with some of my friends. To my amazement, they did seem to get better when I laid hands on them.

'My own healing, and the discovery of healing gifts within myself has led me to research the whole field. I've now been on several spiritual healing courses, I am a member of the National Federation of Spiritual Healers, and have studied the whole field of healing and health.

'I now know that there are ways to gain information other than through the five senses, and that the universe is pulsing with beneficial energy, once we know how to tap into it. I feel now that, through my own illness, I have become a channel for healing. My migraines proved to be the gateway to a whole new outlook and way of life.'

As these case histories show, there is nothing mysterious, nothing esoteric or hidden about personal growth. It is open to all of us to grow, and we all owe it to ourselves to make the most of ourselves. Never before in history has personal growth been so accessible, never has there been so much help for those who wish to make the journey.

The journey is exciting, liberating, empowering. It's also fun. You'll find that a whole new world of interesting things opens up, teases your mind, taxes your intelligence, makes you think. You'll find that life will never seem dull, pointless or boring again, because there is always something new you can try, something which can open and light up yet another corner of your consciousness.

Good luck!

Further Reading

Beattie, Melody, *Codependents' Guide to the Twelve Steps*, Piatkus, 1990.

Bly, Robert, *Iron John*, Element, 1990.

Caddy, Eileen, *Flight into Freedom*, Element, 1990.

Carnes, Patrick, *Don't Call it Love: Recovery from Sexual Addiction*, Piatkus, 1992.

Cassady, Carolyn, *Off the Road*, Flamingo, 1991.

Considine, Mike (ed), *The Whole Person Catalogue*, Brainwave, 1992.

Cunningham, William C, *Empowerment: Vitalizing Personal Energy*, Humanics New Age, 1991.

Dyer, Dr Wayne, *Your Erroneous Zones*, Michael Joseph, 1977.

Grant, Belinda, *A–Z of Natural Health Care*, Optima, 1992.

Grey, Margot, *Return from Death*, Arkana, 1985.

Ferguson, Marilyn, *The Aquarian Conspiracy*, J P Tarcher, 1980.

Hassan, Steven, *Combatting Cult Mind Control*, Thorsons, 1990.

Hay, Louise L, *You Can Heal Your Life*, Eden Grove Editions, 1987.

Hodgkinson, Liz, *The Alexander Technique*, Piatkus, 1987.

Hodgkinson, Liz, *Counselling*, Simon and Schuster, 1992.

Hodgkinson, Liz, *Obsessive Love*, Piatkus, 1992.

Humphreys, Christmas, *Buddhism*, Penguin, 1975.

Jeffers, Susan, *Feel the Fear and Do it Anyway*, Arrow, 1988.

Krystal, Phyllis, *Cutting the Ties that Bind*, Element, 1988.

Marlow, Mary Elizabeth, *Handbook for the Emerging Woman*, Donning, 1988.

Masson, Jeffrey, *Against Therapy*, Fontana, 1989.

McLean, Dorothy, *To Hear the Angels Sing*, Morningtown, 1980.

Pedler, Kit, *The Quest for Gaia*, Souvenir, 1979.

Schaef, Anne Wilson, *When Society Becomes an Addict*, Thorsons, 1992.

Stafford, David, and Hodgkinson, Liz, *Codependency*, Piatkus, 1991.

Schumacher, E C, *Small is Beautiful: Economics as Though People Mattered*, Abacus, 1974.

Silva, José, *The Silva Mind Control Method*, Grafton, 1980.

Index

Index